To Marilyn.

HOW TO PRODUCE A PLAY
for the Amateur Stage

This might be "coals to Newcastle" but
I felt it would add to your collection of
paperbacks & if it tells you nothing you
didn't know already about drama, it might
tell you something about your Mum.
lots of love.
7. 10. 90.

Doris M. Day

Other Allison & Busby 'Writers' Guides'

HOW TO PRODUCE A PLAY

for the Amateur Stage

Doris M. Day

ALLISON & BUSBY

An Allison & Busby book
Published in 1990 by
W. H. Allen & Co. Plc
Unit 26, Grand Union Centre,
338 Ladbroke Grove,
London W10 5AH

Phototypeset by Input Typesetting Ltd, London
Printed in Great Britain by
Cox & Wyman Ltd, Reading, Berks.

ISBN 0 74900 085 6

ACKNOWLEDGEMENTS

The Author and Publishers wish to acknowledge with gratitude the following for permission to use material in which they hold the copyright: the Lucy Kroll Agency of New York for extracts from *The Young Elizabeth* by Jeanette Dowling and Francis Letton; Faber and Faber Ltd, for extracts from *Enter A Free Man* by Tom Stoppard; Sir Stephen Spender and Ed Victor Ltd, for extracts from *Mary Stuart* by Friedrich Schiller, freely translated and adapted by Sir Stephen Spender; Heinemann Publishers (Oxford) Ltd, for extracts from *A Man For All Seasons* by Robert Bolt; and Christopher Fry for extracts from his play *A Phoenix Too Frequent*, all enquiries for which should be made to Actac Ltd, 15 High Street, Ramsbury, Wilts SN8 2PA.

Contents

FOREWORD

The number of people in Britain actively involved in amateur drama is greater than the number who watch football matches. I personally know almost 300 drama groups and obviously there are many, many more. As with all other popular hobbies and interests, innumerable books are available on the subject of amateur drama. Many are written on one particular aspect, most are very expensive and to read them all would take several years.

As a member of an amateur drama group for well over thirty years, I still have problems resolving the many queries which arise out of producing and directing plays. Not only does this book instruct, but it also provides the quick easy reference so necessary when time is limited and if it does not give the answers to all the questions, it tells where the information can readily be obtained.

Doris M. Day is an experienced actress, director, tutor, lecturer, adjudicator and playwright and her book reflects this experience. It is painstakingly researched and embraces all the ramifications of amateur theatre.

For new Drama groups who know very little and for established groups who want to know more and at the same time improve their standards 'How To Produce A Play For The Amateur Stage' is a veritable mine of information and will certainly lead them in the right direction.

BRENDA NICHOLL
Chairman,
National Drama Festivals Association

AUTHOR'S NOTE

Since theatre work is a creative art it is also an *individual* one and some of my ideas on Production/Direction may not conform to those of other people. I make no excuses – these principles and practices have been formulated by me over a number of years, working as an actress/director in the professional theatre, as a professional director in the amateur theatre, and as a professional critic and adjudicator in both! But as Peter Ustinov said about critics: 'They search for ages for the wrong word which, to give them credit, they usually find!'

Chapter One

'THE BUCK STOPS HERE'

This book is intended to be a text book for the amateur theatre, but that does not mean that it will not aim for professional standards. It sets out to give advice to the amateur director-cum-producer – the 'lord high everything else' – the person of whom it can always be said, 'the buck stops here'.

It might be that this person is entirely new to the task, having been thrown in at the deep end, as it were. He or she may have inadequate facilities for the staging of a production, or a company so inexperienced that it would be wiser if they took up 'tatting'. Too many people think that, because they can walk, talk, and learn lines with a 'reasonable' command, therefore they can act. Unlike the professional theatre, where a ruthless casting Director can say 'Don't call us, we'll call you' to aspiring Thespians, nearly all amateur groups are only too glad to recruit willing bodies, often in a desperate hope that some talent will emerge during rehearsals.

In the exceptions, where talent abounds and auditions are held, ample opportunities are often provided for the study and practice of the craft. Even so, it is essential that players and directors are always aware of the need to study and to continue learning the techniques of all aspects of the theatre.

It is not without relevance that where higher standards *are* achieved, the more talented and the more dedicated theatre enthusiasts are attracted, and the groups are more successful as a result. It is such groups that come to me when I am adjudicating and enquire as to the best methods of improving themselves; it is the weaker ones that often walk away with an attitude of knowing it all.

I remember an instance when I had adjudicated the same team over a period of some years in different Festivals around the country. As they walked away, after rather a weak entry, their Director gave me somewhat desultory thanks for my comments, but added: 'Of course, I never take any notice of adjudications.' I enquired why they bothered to enter Festivals, and he replied: 'It gives other audiences an opportunity to see my work . . . ' He then added: 'I don't think I need an adjudicator to tell me how to do something I've been doing for over twenty years.' 'Ah!' I replied. 'That explains why your work is no better now than it was when I first saw it!' Cruel, but true. One can always learn and should seek the opportunity to do so.

It is in the dedicated groups where one sees enterprise, originality and enthusiasm – and much of this comes from the Director. It is a basic fact that one has to be sure of the rules before one can attempt to break them, and theatre is one art form where the rules can be broken very successfully. In this book I will endeavour to give guidelines to the basic rules of production and direction for those who are new to the art form, and for those who are a little practised.

'To be a Producer is a Profession – to be a Director is an Art!' There is always confusion in some quarters about the difference between the Producer and the Director. These terms are often used in the amateur theatre without exact definition of the task in hand. In the professional theatre, the person responsible for the financial and administrative aspects of play production is generally known as the *Producer*. He or she buys the play script, rents or owns the theatre, raises the money, engages the company and handles all the finances.

The *Director* is responsible for the general interpretation of the script, and for the conduct of all rehearsals. Directors guide the cast, welding all into an artistic and dramatic interpretation. They have less responsibility for the financial or business side of the enterprise.

In the amateur theatre, often both tasks are undertaken by the one person; this is true even in educational circles, although sometimes a committee will adopt responsibility for the various tasks of administration.

The situation has not always been the same; the term Director is a comparatively new one, introduced from America. In England, in the early days of the theatre, the one who undertook the two-fold task was often the author or the leading player, which gave rise to the famous 'actor-manager' of the 19th Century. On many an occasion the rest of the cast were left to their own devices, without being given any direction at all. They all strived to make their own role important, but Heaven help them if they scored any 'points' off the leading 'star' of the day!

It is only in the last 80 years or so that 'Directors' have been introduced into the theatre and have made their presence felt. There is no doubt that where their contribution is of a high standard, they have brought a rich understanding of the dramatic art into our lives.

Ivor Brown (a leading theatre critic of his day) once wrote: 'They must know acting from within, and be perfectly acquainted with its technical difficulties. They must understand the mechanics of the stage. Their chief task is to take a detached view of the point which the author seeks to establish. They must relate the word to the appearance, the

3

idea to the atmosphere, the movement to the scene. They are working accordingly in terms of mind and matter in order to fuse them in the service of the whole artistic conception. Their implements are their own sensibility, the plasticity of others and the mechanical equipment of the playhouse.' These are words which are as applicable today as when they were first written in 1928.

It has been said that a Director should also be a performer, artist, architect and electrician, as well as an expert of history, geography, stage costumes, props and scenery. A thorough understanding of human nature is also needed.

I would add the suggestion that it is a great help to be a cross between a sergeant-major and a comedian.

As I have already mentioned, in the amateur theatre the tasks of Director and Producer are often combined, so I won't complicate the issue further, but for the rest of this book I will refer only to the former title, and so as not to give offence to either sex, I will use the word 'you'. How complicated things can become!

I know that in a democratic society all should have an opportunity to express their opinion, and I certainly accept this principle, but I know from wide experience that it is also necessary for the Director to take firm control once the whole project is underway, hence my comment about sergeant-majors. *Your* name will be on the programme as Director; *you'll* be responsible for the interpretation of the script: the 'buck' stops firmly on *your* shoulders!

A firm discussion with all concerned at the onset of the production process will give them an opportunity to air their views, but it is advisable to discourage an excessive exchange of ideas *during* rehearsals. While directorial control should not be so rigid that it doesn't allow for constructive comment, it is wise to suggest that this should be given in private discussion either prior to, or after, rehearsals. Rehearsal time is very precious and must be well husbanded. All will take their cue from the director, and it is essential that anyone accepting that post is aware of this and is prepared to be dedicated enough to give the entire team a confidence which they sometimes lack.

It is obvious that directors who dither, and are not sure of their approach to the play and its production, will unsettle the company. Flexibility is often essential but even changes must be made with authority.

As for the comedian/comedienne, a successful Director will be aware when tension needs to be eased, when a witty word can stop a flow of anger, when a change of mood can lighten the atmosphere. They will be able to take a joke against themselves, make one if necessary, and, equally effectively, pull the whole group back into self-discipline with a quiet word of command.

One of the problems facing the fairly inexperienced director is the well-meaning 'off stage' directions that are often given to the cast by other members of the group, players, previous directors, etc. Their 'instructions' often conflict with the guidelines taken by the current director, and cause confusion and ill-feeling. Such interference, however well-meaning, must be stamped on at once. Remember my previous note about *open* discussion, and when and where it should take place.

So, all is ready, and I will, in the following chapters, give as many guidelines as possible to the whole pattern of Directing a Play. Before I leave this opening chapter, perhaps a true story to give you pause for thought.

When I was a young actress, and becoming very interested in the art of Directing, a well-known West End Director said to me: 'You do know of course, Doris, that if you direct a play and it is a success, everyone will say "What a

Chapter Two

TAKING STOCK

Before proceeding, it's a good idea to check on the resources available to the Director. Obviously an asset you cannot determine is the amount of dedicated support you are likely to receive, but, in the majority of cases, if you are able to create a spark of enthusiasm within the group, and to keep that spark alive, this spirit of endeavour is very contagious, particularly when dealing with young people.

Equally, if your interest lacks lustre and you present a rather bored exterior, you will find that enthusiasm, however strong at the outset, will soon fade. Your best asset is your own excitement at the whole project. Certainly there are moments when the mood is almost euphoric, a feeling of 75% inspiration and creation, and 25% application of the rules, and there will be other occasions when the spark is barely flickering, 75% application of knowledge and 25% (if you're lucky!) of inspiration. But both moods can prevail and must be taken in your stride.

A Director needs to know what administrative support is available. Will any tasks fall on your shoulders apart from the actual interpretation and presentation of the script? In other words, you should clarify your terms of reference.

What are the financial aspects of the task? Have you to present a budget before venturing far, and is it likely to be accepted? Can you suggest further capital expenditure if the proposed production is more ambitious than ever? Would extra money be available if emergency requirements presented problems, like hiring of extra equipment, etc.?

Who would handle publicity? House Management? If such questions appear irrelevant to the post of Director, I can only assure you that in most Amateur Theatre companies they have very strong significance, and certainly need clarification at the outset. A failure in the organisation of such details *can* and *does* determine the success or failure of a production. The people who provide refreshments and check on the seating are as important as the leading player! No matter how exciting the finished production, there will always be audiences who will recall the cold coffee, the hard chairs and the long queue for the toilets. Lucky is the Director who can start rehearsals without any problems niggling away in the background.

Right! What facilities are available for the presentation? Is the group performing in a village hall, a school, its own theatre or the local professional civic theatre? Has the stage a proscenium arch? Is there an apron, a thrust, or is it theatre-in-the-round?

Each venue will obviously have varying assets – and drawbacks. A different size stage, a differently-equipped stage, some places so small one could hardly swing the proverbial cat; others so large that to present an intimate small cast play upon it would take re-organisation and thought.

What size and shape is the wing space? Or the height of the stage? What colour are the drapes? Where are the traverse curtains? Is there a sky-cloth? Flying facilities? Are the main tabs worked manually? in which case the speed at which they open and close can be controlled, something which is not always the case when they are electrically operated. Is there a stage cloth available?

It is essential that other areas of the stage are equally studied. Is there a communication system between stage and dressing rooms, between stage and lighting and control box?

What lighting equipment is there? You need to know the potential use of the control board, the number of lamps, their definitions: profile, fresnal, flood or special use. Where are they sited? Is it possible for them to be moved to more suitable positions? Are there stage lighting 'dips' (lighting sockets) that could supplement the equipment and allow for the use of practical lamps, i.e. wall lights, standard and table lamps, fires, etc.?

Above all, is there a competent operator for the equipment and what is his/her potential as a lighting designer, one with flair and imagination, one who will co-operate with a director?

What equipment is available for the creation of sound effects, and for their amplification? Are there operators available and what is their potential? Are there facilities for an orchestra if required?

What dressing room accommodation is available and how is it equipped? It will be useless considering a large cast production where a great deal of body make-up is required and many costume-changes, if the cast are herded together like cattle.

Has the company a well-equipped wardrobe, which is in the charge of a truly interested and capable person, with capable assistants?

Has the company a stock of scenery including flats, rostra, steps, doors, windows, etc.? Is there a really enthusiastic stage carpenter available, leading an equally enthusiastic team? Have they anywhere to work? Is there among them someone who is capable of designing sets and detail pieces? Similarly, are there any company props and is there anyone who would be interested in creating some items, or collecting them from various sources? In schools and colleges, such talent abounds among the staff.

I firmly believe that such interested persons should be encouraged to demonstrate their talents; many a spark has been quenched for lack of opportunity. To companies that have these various tasks sorted out, these questions may seem irrelevant, but it is important that as the Director you know exactly what the situation is, or you will be left at the last moment trying to do too many 'off stage' tasks.

It is, of course, absolutely essential that there is a reliable stage manager who will harness all those technical forces. A stage manager needs to be someone who is very practical, methodical, knowledgeable in the ways of theatre, in the technicalities of the stage; a person who will not panic, is easily adaptable and ingenious, who can wield authority with a great deal of tact, and, like a Director, be a cross between a sergeant-major and a comedian. Strangely enough, such persons do exist!

It is also extremely useful if you are able to appoint a Production Secretary, someone who will liaise between you and the stage manager, the cast, the Administration and House Management; but, best of all, someone who will be prepared to be at your beck and call, sitting beside you, taking notes, someone who is able to interpret your mood. This is also a good opportunity for those who are themselves interested in learning something about directing a play, by becoming a production assistant, (and note, *I do not mean* an assistant Director), but they can at least get the general idea of the processes, if only how *not* to go about it.

Of course, other important commodities are time and space. What rehearsal room is available, when and for how long? How many rehearsals are expected, and how long can they last? When can the cast actually work with the set?

What are the arrangements going to be for the 'get in' and the striking, the 'getting out'?

I am often asked how long should rehearsals take. It's a bit like asking the length of a piece of string: it all depends on the company, the director and the way you work. I would say that usually most groups take far too long. It is much better to have a brisk concentrated rehearsal period than to have it drag on over many weeks. It would really be more advantageous for me to advise the hours that perhaps would be spent in such preparation. One thing I would specify is that no one should ever look on any rehearsal period as a time when lines are learnt. A rehearsal period is just that – a time when any aspect of dialogue and business is *rehearsed*, the dialogue and the business having been learnt previously – but never learnt parrot fashion without knowledge of the setting, the character, relationships and situation. Certainly rehearsal should not go on for so long and late that everyone is exhausted; far better to take more care in the planning. I shall deal with that in a later chapter. Let the directors 'take stock', as I have suggested, and make notes of their discoveries about the resources, make notes of the promises of help they've been given, and plan to call a technical meeting as soon as they've selected the script for their production.

So, armed with this knowledge, aware that you have this or that facility, this assistance, that equipment, all of which can be used to enhance and enrich your work as Director, it's time to decide on the script – but where are the players? What human assets have you?

Your choice of script will certainly be affected by the players that are available: not only their sex, but age, ability and availability. It's no good considering a player for a leading role if he or she hasn't got the time or the dedication necessary.

Another factor that may affect your position as Director is if the company or school administration includes a play selection and a casting committee. In the first instance the play selection committee may suggest a script which is not to your liking, and in these circumstances it would be difficult to enthuse, create, interpret with verve. Similarly, any outside ruling over the casting of a script may seriously affect the interpretation of that script, and directorial control would be difficult to sustain in these conditions; not impossible, but difficult, and that could create problems during rehearsals.

There is no doubt that there are many factors to consider, but these problems are usually sorted out with goodwill, otherwise we would not have the great spirit of amateur theatre which exists today.

And that spirit starts to flicker when a certain decision is made: what will the next play be?

Chapter Three

THE SELECTING OF THE PLAY

I have said that, in some companies, the process of choosing a script depends on a committee who plan for a whole year. They obviously seek a balanced programme which will satisfy and stimulate the audience, give general opportunities to company members and, with luck, be financially viable. This does not usually apply in educational establishments, where other factors such as term time and exams have to be considered. Obviously some productions will be more lavish than others and cost more but do not necessarily draw a larger income, whereas a small budget 'pot boiler' will often be very profitable.

There is bound to be the enthusiast of a particular type of theatre who is keen to introduce something new; someone who wants to suggest a musical despite the fact that none of the members has musical ability; another who wants to do the latest West End comedy, and so on. The theatre spectrum is wide and there are those who want to be courageous in choice, in contrast to those who seek caution.

Whatever the process of selection for a company, one thing is of supreme importance, and that is the fact that the Director must be enthused by the challenge of material offered and should make the final decision. I think this is particularly important in the amateur theatre: in the professional the Director, having had more training and experience, is able to lean heavily on the technique of production and direction, and their fellow professionals will help to create the essential magic that gets the adrenalin working.

One problem that faces the amateur is the actual opportunity of obtaining scripts to read, and maybe discarding them till the right one is found. It is obvious that by supporting other groups and as much professional theatre as possible, one is introduced to a wide variety of writing. Reading theatre criticisms and making a note of those that appeal is another method; visiting Drama Festivals to watch entries from a wide area is also an ideal way to see plays and to collect ideas.

County Drama Libraries vary, but many have a very wide selection of scripts of all kinds, and enquiries at the local branch will give information about the catalogues. Organisations like the British Theatre Association, the Drama Associations of Wales and Scotland, and the National Operatic and Dramatic Association have lending library facilities and will certainly advise on the subject.

Theatre magazines like the quarterly *Drama* devote space to the reviewing of new plays, as does *Amateur Stage*. This latter is a monthly magazine which not only contains such useful data, but will also publicise your forthcoming production. Since it is published particularly for amateur enthusiasts, it is also a fund of general theatre information.

Play publishers will also supply catalogues which give a brief synopsis of their publications and in some cases there are facilities where you can sit and browse through any that may interest you. To wade through possible scripts does take time; there are many factors to consider. By now, however, the Director is armed with knowledge of the resources available and should have some idea of the type of script required.

14

HOW TO PRODUCE A PLAY

What makes a good play? This is a question that I, as an adjudicator, am often asked, and obviously I have to reply, 'It all depends –'

I use the term 'play', for though the libretto of a musical *is* important, the lyrics and the musical score form such a large part of the whole that the story becomes almost a peg on which to hang the music.

It isn't necessary for the storyline to have a beginning, a middle and an end, but I do think it helps, particularly when dealing with a fairly inexperienced group. It helps them to understand the 'shape' of the play and the developments of the plot. However, one should always remember that there are strong and sound pieces of writing for the theatre which are almost formless, but which nevertheless have great impact when played and presented with strength. Take, for instance, the works of Beckett, Pinter, Ionesco, etc, the Theatre of the Absurd; the Theatre of Menace.

The script should be based on strength, a firm framework, even if the theme appears to be obscure. In a realistic play, the dramatic 'shape' needs to be clearly defined, even allowing for the twists of the sub-plots. The characters should be of sound depth, and credible. A good writer has a skill in translating the banalities of everyday dialogue into effective language, which still does not appear to be false to the characters or their origins. Remember, sound acting is based on the ability to present characters with truth.

It is essential for the Director to be aware of the author's intention. Was his purpose merely to entertain, or are there more serious implications? Was his purpose to stimulate argument, or political or social awareness? These things should be clear. A confused Director will lead no-one to a satisfactory understanding, even of the writings of a confused author!

Into which convention, Theatrical or Naturalistic, does

15

the play fit? In other words, is it a piece of writing that reflects life in a realistic fashion, where the setting, presentation and performance must be truthful to the circumstances and characters? Or does the writing suggest a world where theatrical invention and imagination can be brought into play; where a suggestion of a property, a light, can suggest a whole scene; where fantasy can replace fact?

In the first instance, let us look at a comedy by Bill Naughton called *Spring and Port Wine*. It is set in the home of a working-class family in Bolton, Lancashire. The family is ruled by the father, the mother is frightened of contravening his principles; yet there is love and affection in the house. The characters are well-researched, the situation very credible, even an amusing neighbour never goes beyond the outline of character, never developing into a caricature. There is underlying tragedy and during the course of the play innermost feelings are revealed, but there is a happy ending. There is truth in the situation, the character, the dialogue and the developments of the plot. Therefore, the performance, presentation and production must reflect that truth. Any introduction of fantasy would destroy it.

Similar treatment is essential for J. B. Priestley's *An Inspector Calls* even though we finally realise that the Inspector is, in fact, a metaphysical figure, seeming to strike the consciences of the family over the death of a girl, yet in fact never actually arriving at the house at all. Any attempt to make a 'spirit' figure of the man would nullify the purpose of the playwright.

In the convention of theatricality, there is every excuse for 'licence' in production and performance, provided everyone is sure as to the *extent of freedom*. In Peter Brook's production of *A Midsummer Night's Dream* the normally accepted presentation was altered radically to that of a circus ring, with trapeze brought into play. Thus the interpretation of the script was given entirely new dimensions. While the invention of the production may have offended purists, many audiences found the project exciting, but each and every one connected with the production was aware of the limits to which they could go and the form in which they had to work.

In seeking a play, a director should not be scared of tackling a script which may appear to present problems of technical presentation. A call for several scene changes can often be solved quite easily with a little thought, even on a small stage. Multi-purpose locations can be achieved with careful planning. The use of 'skeleton sets', 'detail screens', spotlit areas, etc. will be accepted by the audience quite happily if production and performance are strong.

There are many instances where the conventions can be mixed, where inventive directors will combine all aspects to create a fantasy, or introduce symbolic elements which will provide a simple solution to what could be a complicated piece of staging.

For instance, leaving aside the political symbolism of a play like *The Caucasian Chalk Circle* by Bertolt Brecht, the script deals mainly with the kidnapping of a child, for its own good, by a young servant girl. She travels far and wide and experiences many trials before she finally faces the child's mother. The action requires the setting of many scenes. Her travels take her over mountains, broken bridges and streams, the presentation of which could present insoluble problems if attempts were made to be completely realistic in the detail. Theatrical licence must be brought into use. Yet it is also essential for the characters to be sincerely and truthfully presented, and for the situation in which they find themselves to be honestly shown. The mountains can be suggested by rostra, the bridge over a chasm a

17

mere rope stretched between the rostra, or the stream a rippling piece of cloth, but if the mood is strong in creation, these simple devices will be accepted by the audience without reserve.

Another example – *Habeas Corpus* by Alan Bennett. This script is a satirical 'merry-go-round' based on the satisfaction of sexual passion, where the permissive society is taken to task. Three chairs on a bare stage are called upon to represent both interior and exterior locations. The dialogue covers prose and poetry, the characters border (but only just) caricature; movements must be choreographed as the cast 'dance' their way through their sexual encounters. This is a play, therefore, which can use theatrical device and invention to highlight the author's sense of satirical fantasy.

Simple devices too, can be used to hoodwink the public equally effectively. I recall directing a comedy called *Say Who You Are* by Keith Waterhouse and Willis Hall. In this there are several locations, on different levels, and a lift in constant use between them. Obviously this is not a practical proposition on many stages, but a door to a curtained area, and a cleverly placed set of lights to suggest the reaching of several floors, did the trick, so much so that various members of the audience asked the House Manager how deep the lift dropped below the stage.

Theatrical trickery maybe, but in seeking a play, it is essential to know the rules of convention so that they can be adjusted where required.

Directors no doubt will have some idea of the genre of play they are seeking. A large proportion of amateur companies favour comedies – 'Everyone likes a laugh' they say, but they often forget that true comedy requires a great deal of technical skill. The amusing scene which looks so easy, is usually the one that creates the most problems. There is an old saying 'Comedy is a serious business' and that is very true. It requires a sound knowledge of the technique of timing, both physically and vocally. It requires an ability to stand back, without any emotional involvement, and assess the value of a performance clinically, so that the maximum laughter is achieved *when it is intended*. Never should laughs be derived at the expense of the player, only of the character.

All should be able to define the various classes of comedy. Generally, there is the natural comedy, where laughter is achieved because of human frailty and the situations in which the characters are placed. There is an underlying tragedy in such work, which sparks off the situation, and therefore realism is all-important.

Take, for instance, the comedy *Sailor Beware* by Philip King and Falkland Cary. One of the main characters is the termagant of a mother. She rides roughshod over her husband, her sister-in-law, her daughter and her daughter's fiancé, and most of the humour is derived from their frenzied attempts either to placate or to avoid her. In truth, it is a sorry household, yet because it is a situation which is possible, we identify with them and laugh at their efforts.

In a comedy of manners, *style* is all-important. While the characters are realistic, the situation equally so, the presentation of characters in speech, movement and gesture requires a slight artificiality because of the façade behind which they hide. An example is Restoration Comedy, where a false exterior is presented together with the wigs, the exaggeration of costume and make-up. Again a certain degree of style and artificiality is necessary when involved with High Comedy classics such as *The Importance of Being Earnest* by Oscar Wilde. The characters in this instance hide behind a façade because of the conventions of the society in which they live.

In tackling black comedy, the Director needs to be aware

that it is the macabre quality of the situation that is the fulcrum of the laughter. A good example is Joe Orton's play *Loot*, where a coffin hides the proceeds of a robbery, and false grief hides greed and sexual proclivity.

Farce is surely the most demanding category of comedy. It is an extreme form where laughter is raised at the expense of probability. The situation is improbable, but not impossible. Here a good example is *Hotel Paradiso* by the French playwright Feydeau. In this, M. Boniface, an architect, plans an illicit stay at the hotel, with his neighbour's wife, while his own wife is away. The neighbour, M. Cot, who is an inspector of plumbing, also comes to the hotel; likewise his nephew, who has been enticed there by the architect's maid. Another visitor is M. Martin and his four young daughters. All is confusion and muddled identity, sub-plots abound; there is a police raid and the inevitable, hilarious chase in and out of the bedrooms and staircases of the building. The characters are characters – a capital 'C' perhaps – but they should not become Caricatures. Directional control must be firm to avoid any degeneration into burlesque.

In any form of comedy, there is always the danger of the extrovert player going 'over the top' with ad-libs and the inclusion of extraneous bits of business. Any excessive emotion displayed in a drama will be equally risky. This element should be avoided at all costs. Such behaviour ruins the production and makes for great difficulty for all other people concerned. The rest of the cast are usually left standing 'with egg on their faces'.

Perhaps a thriller is what is being sought; if so, then the Director should make sure that the characters are true and well-presented in the writing, and that the plot is strong enough to thrill. So often, what has appeared to be dramatically sound collapses when the third act is written. Often too, there are so many 'red herrings' that the audience, when they have time for analysis (during the intervals, for instance) can pick holes in the whole fabric of the script.

Perhaps the 'Classics' are being considered. This is a term which is used freely in the theatre, but which creates much misunderstanding. Generally, a 'classic' is a piece of writing that has stood the test of time, that has been accepted as having literary (or musical) merit. Under this heading would come the work of such playwrights as Shakespeare, Marlowe, Sophocles, Aristophanes, Ibsen, Chekhov, Oscar Wilde – to name but a few.

Their work should certainly be studied and considered; many amateurs tend to shun them for various reasons, often because of the problems of casting. Many of the earlier works were written at a time when few women were used as players, and therefore they require a large cast of males. One financial advantage of doing such a play is that, almost without exception, if the writer has been dead over fifty years, there is no royalty to pay. The exception being if the script you are using is a more modern adaptation of the original, and the adaptor is alive, or only deceased *within* the last fifty years.

Another option is to tackle the script which deals with fact: the historical, the documentary, the biography, etc. These can be very rewarding, but they do require a great deal of research into the characters and the situation. Obviously the writer has done *his/her* work in the compilation of the script, but in the actual presentation and performance it is essential to verify certain details to ensure verisimilitude, and such research is of extreme advantage to all concerned.

To go from one extreme to another, the Company may want to perform a theatrical piece of entertainment such as a revue, a pantomime or a musical. It is important again that the script is a sound one. In the case of the Pantomime, a traditional story is at stake, and I feel it is as important as the comic 'business' and songs that are the common link. The dialogue is adjustable, according to the prevailing local or national situation. This allows for the 'in'-joke, topical and satirical, usually at the expense of politicians, or pop stars, or even the company members themselves. Basically, however, the thrills of the storyline should prevail.

Where Revue is concerned, the jokes should be strong, the dialogue witty, the lyrics slick, the music catchy. The demands are the same whether the aim is satirical or bawdy!

Then to the Musical – only too often, the old favourites come trotting out and yet *they* can hardly be called 'Classics' in either the literary or the musical sense! The storyline is often so weak as to be almost non-existent, the jokes stale, the characters without depth or feeling. I feel that groups need to be more ambitious in their selection, not in the lavishness of production costs, but in trying to introduce their public to a wider variety of musical show.

Finally, there is the unscripted material, the improvisation where a theme is discussed or researched by the group of players themselves. Many theatre projects have their origins in this fashion; it is a process that can be rewarding or time-wasting – *it all depends*. Certainly the same rules of strength apply. I would not recommend the inexperienced Director to jump into the deep end with such fragile material, but for those who know the rules sufficiently to break them, it is another matter altogether.

So. As a Director you 'pays your money and you takes your choice' . . . and by now your senses should be tingling with anticipation and a feeling of 'let's go!'

However, before you get too involved, you'd better check with the publishers of your chosen script to make sure a 'licence to perform' is available. Remember that if a professional production is planned, permission is not always available for amateur companies to do the same. I have known several groups who have fallen unwittingly into that trap: having planned a rehearsal and even advertised such a production, they find it is illegal according to the licensing laws which govern these affairs. This occurred recently when a school planned and rehearsed a production of *West Side Story* only to find that they were refused the rights, since a professional West End production had been proposed.

Now is the time to check; that's a task for that production secretary – before it's too late. Then, we can really start the ball rolling.

Chapter Four

THE DIRECTOR'S APPROACH TO THE PLAY

While it is important to obtain swift co-operation from the technical and administrative staff, it is vital that they have a sound understanding of the script and its demands. Obviously the same principle applies to the Director. How otherwise can you be sure of the demands that you are going to make on all concerned?

A Director needs to be absolutely sure of the details of the script to be an authority on the subject. This authority will be questioned throughout the rehearsal period. 'Why is X going out through *that* door?', or even more tricky 'What's she doing while she's out there?' A piece of dramatic writing deals with a situation within a given period of time, and a director needs to be aware of all that happens within that time span. If you have to invent an answer, it should at least be credible, and such invention will often help to settle the mind of a puzzled player who needs to know exactly what he or she is doing and why.

Likewise, confidence will be a source of strength when dealing with technical staff, who often query every demand. Frequently the Director will tell the Stage Manager what he wants, and the Stage Manager will tell him what he's going to get! While compromise is often necessary, you should allow the technical staff to win *some* of the battles, but you must ensure that you win the war.

Certainly by now, you should be aware of the genre, the convention and the writer's intention. It is, therefore, worth your while to continue the study of the script to gain further information. I would recommend that notes taken at this stage will be a great asset later, and will save time and argument.

So, what are you looking for? Which notes are going to be valuable? –

A. *The storyline and the developments of the plots and sub-plots*. This needs to be succinct and clear. (See later synopsis of imaginary script.)
B. *The Dramatic 'shape' of the play*. Care in studying this will provide a 'graph' and will demonstrate a pattern of the tempo of the developments. To obtain this, it is essential to research what I call the three 'C's. **CONTRAST . . . CONFLICT . . . and CLIMAX**.

For example:–
1. Contrasts within the situations at any given moment.
2. Contrasts between the characters and their intentions.
3. Contrasts between the characters and their relationships.
4. Contrasts in the *created* mood.

1. Conflicts *within* the situation at any given moment.
2. Conflicts *within* the characters. (Their internal pressures.)
3. Conflicts *between* the characters.
4. Conflicts *within* the relationships.

1. The Climax of any scene that happens during the course of the play.
2. The Final Climax of the development of the situation.

For the moment let us study an 'Imaginary' play and its synopsis.

MARY is sweet, apparently undemanding of life and her fellow creatures, *but* she has a secret hold over MARTHA (the latter having had an abortion in the past).

MARTHA is apparently bitter and hostile *but* it is a façade which hides her sadness and frustration.

They are both in love with JOHN, a fine, upstanding man who is a fellow servant at the country mansion owned by their employer RALPH, who is a successful writer *but* who has for some time been losing money gambling.

JOHN is flattered by the attentions of the two maids *but* is in love with his employer's secretary, JANE.

She appears to be quiet, efficient, good-natured *but*, in the past, has been successfully prosecuted for embezzlement. She is now living at the mansion, working for RALPH under an assumed name.

In the first act, the characters and the basic situation are introduced. There is little dramatic action apart from a row between MARTHA and JANE over some missing money. MARY commiserates with JANE but, as the act finishes, she is beginning to be suspicious of the secretary's past.

In the second act JOHN reveals his love for JANE to MARY, but MARTHA overhears and, misunderstanding, wrongly believes him to love MARY. As the act finishes, MARY is discovered dead in bed – apparently from an overdose of drugs.

In the third act JANE is accused of murder; the police

26

suspecting that blackmail was the motive. JANE has an alibi (she had spent the night with John). Accusations are levelled at MARTHA, but she is able to reveal the truth. RALPH was the murderer: he was involved with the drug trade in an attempt to recoup his losses. MARY had discovered this and had been blackmailing him!

Now, a careful study of the graph overleaf reveals the dramatic 'shape' of the play, the lines moving left being the normal tempo of general conversation, those moving right the increased tempo, of tension, anger, excitement, etc.

Obviously, this is an extreme example and there are, in every script, many more subtle twists that need consideration.

C. *The presentation and staging of the script.*
1. Does this call for specialised research in any field?
2. Is the setting going to be a problem?

By now you should also have some ideas of the kind of setting the script demands, and your own ideas about the staging you are seeking. Likewise with sound effects and lighting, etc., and you should start making some sketches and notes on the subject. This is where prior knowledge of the resources available is a boon, and you are not working 'in limbo', as it were.

D. *The period of the play.* It may be that further historical research is necessary to guarantee accuracy in presentation and performance.

Before proceeding, I'd like to suggest the 'jigsaw puzzle' as a general symbolism for a director to follow. When tackling this kind of diversion one is always very well aware of the

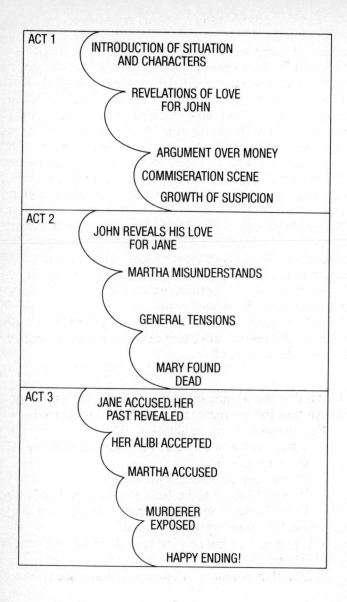

picture, studying it, assessing its attraction for you and for other people. You have a good look at it before you buy it, and another study is made before you start to do it.

First you empty out the box; ensure that you have enough working space to complete it. The picture (the script) is there to guide you, and gradually the pieces are collated and joined together to make a composite whole. If the pieces aren't correct, they will not fit – thus it is essential that *your* pieces, i.e. notes, etc., are complete and sound. Gradually, and *not attempting too much at a time*, the picture is completed.

Many of the 'pieces' deal with the nature of the characters, their case histories, their purposes and intentions, their relationships. Playwrights give little information on the frontispiece. They might say 'Mary Brown is a maid, aged 25', but that's all – so much more comes to light when a close study is made of the script.

I would suggest this approach, not only for the Director, but for all the cast as well, and prior to rehearsal. Again it calls for note-taking, of:-

1. All that the author says about the character.
2. All that the character reveals about him/herself.
   For instance, Mary might say:
      'I was always a shy girl at school. I hate meeting new people.' Or,
      'I never wanted to be a maid.' Or,
      'Why did I have to be born into a poor family?' or,
      'I was in bed early last night. I heard nothing.' –
      What do these speeches reveal?
3. All that other characters reveal about the one in question:
      (Another servant) 'You should have seen the way

she treated her mother. I wouldn't have believed it
of her.'
(Martha) 'She was always the sweet, shy one, but
she'd never share anything.'
(John) 'I've seen her talking to Ralph Smith a
number of times lately – and looking very pleased
with herself afterwards.'
(Jane) 'I don't care what Martha says, she couldn't
have been more pleasant to me when I first came
here to work.'

Note the conflicts and contrasts in these statements. On the
skeletal framework of such information is the truth of the
character built. The exterior, the speech, movement and
gesture are developed and then further study can fill in the
personal image, the make-up, the hairstyle and the clothes.

The next stage is to face the casting of the play. The Director
is aware of the talent available (or lack of it), and the
characters that are required. There are often many
extraneous problems that will affect the issue.

Is it wise or politic to give the leading roles to those most
experienced, who always appear in the company productions, or is now the time to give an opportunity to a
lesser-known player? I am not in favour of a practice that
creates a 'star' system. This can often lead to discontent
among the regular stalwarts, and the 'star' can often prove
temperamental and refuse to accept less than the lead.

In the professional world of theatre it is a different matter,
for there is more scope, a wider range of players available.
It is a Director's market. A 'star' name, if the finances
can stretch that far, is often an attraction that can make a
theatrical venture a viable and profitable one.

In the amateur theatre, this is rarely the case, and there

are many issues to be balanced. For example, we all know that if an experienced player is not used there is always the danger that he or she will defect to another group.

I am a great believer in the creation of an 'ensemble' where the *company* is important and where everyone is prepared to work in any capacity, in an effort to improve the standard of the production. That means being prepared to tackle *any* task onstage, backstage and in the administration of the Front of House. However, everyone's circumstances are different, and it is not for others to dictate, only to comment!

But to the casting. A Director should try to avoid the constant cliché of typecasting, and should be prepared to experiment and stretch the knowledge and talent of all players.

Age is a problem. While many players are able credibly to portray characters older than themselves, it is a rare talent that can successfully 'knock off' more than a few years. Not only is the facial appearance to be considered, but the general physical aspect. These are factors to be considered, though they can be adjusted with care, study and technique.

Personality is important. One needs a presence that can be communicated to the audience. Vocal ability is a must. A variation of tonal qualities (particularly among women) will keep alive the spark of interest and avoid monotony.

Reliability is a quality we discussed in a previous chapter; while it is not easy to assess on first acquaintance, time will tell and it is an essential part of a player's contribution.

Sometimes a Director is able to have a choice, in which case you will no doubt call for auditions, and here it is a good idea not only to ask the candidates to read parts of the play, but to select another piece from an entirely different genre; get them to do a brief improvisation, perhaps, not on their own, but with several other people. This is an excellent opportunity to assess other aspects of performance: stage presence, flexibility of movement, a quick mind. It gives an opportunity to see the contrasts of figure and voice, and to note the enthusiasm towards the art form. There is, to be perverse, the player who auditions badly, but develops wonderfully as rehearsals proceed!

So the cast has been chosen, and given the opportunity to form their own opinions. The script can be studied and preliminary discussions organised, during which the Director's approaches are outlined, everyone being given the opportunity to understand how the script is going to be interpreted, to argue their own viewpoints, to make excuses and what have you, to ask their many questions. So it's all go, or is it?

Isn't it about time to get the Administration Staff and the Technicians on to that rolling ball?

Chapter Five

'FOR WANT OF A NAIL . . . '

While I appreciate the fact that drama groups, schools, etc., all work under differing conditions, there are certain problems that affect them all. I am aware that there are many societies whose standard is of the highest, whose approach to acting, production, presentation and administration is extremely efficient. This book is aimed at those who are *trying* to be all those things, but who need a little guidance.

In the former instance, the Director is unlikely to be concerned with problems of Administration, but only too often, as I said in the opening chapter 'The Buck Stops Here', you are called upon to be 'head cook and bottle washer'. A production secretary is certainly a great asset in such circumstances.

Let us look at the problems of Administration that may face such a person. *It all depends* – on the conditions under which the group work: their finances, their numbers, where they are located (in a town or in a small village), whether they have their own premises for rehearsal and production, or have to resort to hiring them.

Booking of Premises

This may involve two separate issues, premises for rehearsal, plus premises for actual production. This needs to be done at the earliest stage, sometimes even months before rehearsals start. Halls get booked up very early, and it will be too late if other plans are already under way.

If a contract is involved, it is imperative that this is closely studied to ensure that the terms laid down are suitable, and also important to retain copies of all agreed factors, such as:

a. The times the premises are to be used, as well as the dates, and whether overtime is likely to be charged.

b. The arrangements for access. Is a key given, or are arrangements to be made with a caretaker? Are they likely to be flexible in their attitude to times? It must be remembered that such people work long hours during the day, and are as anxious to get home as others.

c. The seating capacity of the building. Are seats already in situ? If not, who is responsible for this task? Do the seats need to be locked together? Are there facilities for disabled members of the audience?

d. What heating is available? What lighting? Is the use of the stage allowed during rehearsals? What storage room is there for set, props, etc.? And what kind of dressing room and toilet accommodation is there?

e. Are the premises registered for public performances, music and dancing?

f. What insurance cover is included in the Contract? e.g. Public liability; personal injury; property loss, etc. (remember that valuable and sometimes irreplaceable props may be loaned by cast and supporters). If this is not sufficient, then additional cover may be required.

g. Check the fire regulations governing *all* that takes place on the premises, and the supply of fire-fighting equipment.

h. Is the use of kitchen and bar included in the hire charge? Who provides the staff for these? Who supplies the refreshments? Who takes the profit?

i. Are there any stage and lighting plans available? Which of these facilities are to be used under the contract?

j. Does the contract include the services of any professional stage staff? If so, when are they available for discussion and planning? Are they limited by Trade Union rules in their co-operation?

k. What parking facilities are available, not only for the public, but for the company and for the transport that is going to deliver and take away the sets, etc.?

l. Ensure that arrangements for the 'Get In' and the 'Get Out', the setting and striking of a show are covered *and confirmed*.

m. Confirm the charge for the entire operation and whether a deposit has to be paid. The costs of this section will form a large share of the budget.

n. Confirm responsibility for the condition of the building after the show. (Some theatres will charge for cleaning services.)

Hall Manager and Staff

County Officers will usually supply on request a copy of rules and regulations appertaining to a particular building.

The contract for a theatre will usually reveal these in the small print, and they must be adhered to.

a. Regulations under the Safety Provisions often state the minimum number of attendants required, plus the House Manager.
b. Early attendance of stewards is called for, usually at least one hour before the opening of the show.
c. Each person is called upon to be responsible for a section of the audience, and to be thoroughly acquainted with all safety precautions, emergency exits, etc.
d. No steward to be under the age of 16 years, or disabled in any way.

Failure to comply with regulations can give the Safety Officer the right to stop performances immediately. These conditions *may* be less stringent in public halls, schools, etc., but it is wise to check early in the proceedings.

Box Office

It may be that members of the company are themselves responsible for this task, particularly if they are performing in their own premises or local halls. In this instance, they no doubt have their own system for the sale of tickets both before and during the run of the show.

If seats are to be reserved, with all seating numbered, then it is essential that seating plans are available and that a competent Box Office Manager ensures that there are no complications of double booking, etc. Some Little Theatres, such as the Millar Centre at Caterham, have a sound supporters' group including many retired people. They undertake many tasks for the theatre, including manning the Box Office during the day, and this certainly helps the stability of the revenue.

If the theatre is a professional one, its Box Office staff will handle ticket sales for the hiring company. In this instance, however, you may find that the actual tickets have to be supplied in four fold, giving four stubs, two for the member of the public (one of which will be taken by the usher on duty prior to the performance, and the other retained), the third for theatre tax records, and the last for retention in case of query. Such tickets cost more to print, but the theatre can often get these printed cheaply since they order in quantity.

Where the theatre does offer a ticket sales service, it will usually charge a commission, somewhere in the region of 10% or slightly more.

The price charged for seats is entirely up to the group. *It all depends* – on the cost of production and the group's policy in this respect. Often concessions are allowed to students, pensioners, and for party bookings.

The Publicity Officer

A good Publicity Officer is a gem indeed. They need to have nerves of steel, to be extrovert and inventive, with a receptive mind and a good ear for the titbit of news that might attract publicity. They also need to have friends in high places – such as in the local newspaper offices, local radio, local shops, county offices, libraries, the Rotary Club, Round Table, Women's Institute, Townswomen's Guild, schools, factories, etc., etc.

There is an old saying that there's no such thing as bad publicity. Remember how Peter O'Toole was vilified by theatre critics for his performance as *Macbeth* at the Old Vic?

'O'Toole "staggers" round the stage as if he were spitting out a list of words he'd inadvertently swallowed.'

'Macbeth staggers from the murder chamber drenched in enough gore to service a blood transfusion unit after a twenty car pile-up on the M.1.'

'O'Toole delivers every line with a monotonous tenor bark as if he were addressing an audience of Eskimos who had never heard of Shakespeare . . . '

Despite such bitter blows, however, they did not prove to be fatal – indeed the public thronged to the theatre each night to judge for themselves!

Newspapers and local radio are interested in *News*, not the bare fact that 'The Players Plentiful are presenting *East Lynne* at such and such a place and time on such and such a day.' This offered information is usually 'spiked' and forgotten, or tucked away in an odd corner between the reports of a funeral and a jumble sale. They will be interested in the fact that 'the leading man has postponed his wedding in order to concentrate on rehearsals, etc . . . ' or 'the Rev. Eli Brown will be doing a strip tease on stage every night as part of his role in *Charley's Aunt*'. That's news and headline material.

Under the heading of publicity, is the ordering of the printing: tickets, posters, leaflets, programmes, etc. The amount of money spent on these items again will be reflected in the budget and it all depends on company policy. I think that, in the main, most amateur companies tend to 'penny pinch', though I do appreciate that you can't spend what you haven't got. But there is also the argument that you have to speculate to accumulate! Cheap, skimpy posters, etc., will attract no one; they give a cheap look to the whole venture. Equally important, I would remind you that glossy paper alone will not sell tickets.

However, good, well-designed posters, on carefully selected sites will at least draw attention to the project. A plentiful supply of leaflets (smaller editions of the posters) are very useful. They can be left in shops, surgeries, libraries, factory canteens, etc., sent to local organisations such as I have listed elsewhere, and distributed door to door by members of the company living in various areas; they are an asset when trying to sell tickets, and naturally the personal approach is the most advantageous. A wise method is to hand out a leaflet, introduce a personal note about the company and the production, and follow it up! If the response looks promising, clinch the deal at the time; if there is a note of hesitancy, follow it up a little later. Practice will soon educate the seller as to the exact likelihood of making a sale. Beware of too much unwelcome pressure – that can put someone off entirely.

Where posters are exhibited, it is often worthwhile to offer complimentary tickets to the displayer. Not only does this introduce new people to the productions, but the displayers are often in a position to introduce complete strangers to future productions. A friendly contact by the Publicity Officer will do nothing but good in these circumstances.

Likewise, other 'agents' in various areas can be contacted, asked to publicise and sell tickets for a production, and given some suitable reward for their services, e.g. a small commission, or free tickets.

Photograph displays of the cast, set, scenes from the play, etc. are always of great interest to the general public, and if it is possible to have them well-sited prior to the show, they will help to 'spread the word'. When sending photographs for reproduction to newspapers, magazines, or to printers handling the programmes, it is wise to check, *before* the film is taken, if black and white or colour prints are to be supplied.

The type of programme supplied is dictated by the policy of the group and their finances. To be frank, most programmes are sold in the ratio of one to every three members of the audience, and are usually discarded after the show, though a few may be preserved as souvenirs. I have seen plain broad sheets giving the bare facts of cast, technical staff, time and locale of production, etc. given away freely, and the gesture is appreciated.

At the other end of the spectrum is the elaborate, glossy eight-fold programme containing, in addition to the bare facts, photographs, lists of previous productions, lists of patrons, etc. They cost more and sell for a higher price. They also contain plenty of advertising matter, obviously a welcome source of revenue to offset the costs; but do remember that someone has to sell that space, and it takes time and courage!

Refreshments

This aspect would appear not to be the concern of the Director, but you would be well-advised to display some interest. For one thing, the people responsible will need to know the number, approximate time, and length of the intervals at which this facility is to be provided. It is also advisable to give them some idea of the size of the audiences for which they will have to cater. Obviously, co-operation between them and the Hall Manager should sort that problem each night. An efficient production secretary should settle all questions of this nature.

In Chapter Two, I mentioned the effect of cold coffee on the audience. I would like to add a few personal experiences I have suffered while attending shows as a member of the audience: a little reflection on these would do no harm.

In the first instance, the coffee was being served on trays by attendants, *direct to the seated and therefore captive audience*. While other people were moving about trying to get to the toilets, it proved to be a hazardous business. I was scalded as the tray tipped and the contents fell in my lap.

At the same Little theatre, we were served so late that the second act was spoilt for all as frantic attempts were made by the same attendants to collect the empties. The chatter, whispers and clink of china proved to be a great distraction.

In the third instance, the intervals were so short, barely ten minutes, the refreshment staff so inadequate, likewise the toilet facilities, that the audience were either fuming at not being served, or having to make a decision between comfort and coffee, as they were faced with the hot coffee and did not have time to drink it. Again the second act was marred as the stragglers fought their way back to their seats.

A question of Director's responsibility? Maybe not, but poor Administration certainly. For the want of a nail a shoe was lost, for the want of a shoe a horse was lost, for the want of a horse a rider was lost and who knows, maybe a Crown!

Talking about nails, we should now look at the 'nuts and bolts' of the technical problems of production.

Chapter Six

THE NUTS AND BOLTS

The natural progression from 'the want of a nail' is a consideration of the 'nuts and bolts', and that term certainly sums up the activities of the backstage staff, the technical crew. Since they must form a sound basis for your production, it is essential to confirm at the outset their terms of reference, to discuss openly with them your interpretation of the script, and what you are seeking in the manner of their contribution.

It is not within the purpose of this book to venture far into the mechanics of these backstage activities, but the work of the Director is impossible without their assistance. Like the cast, they should have had an opportunity to study the script of the proposed production, and to understand the problems of its presentation.

Harold Melvill tells of a time when he was a scenic artist with a repertory company at Rochester. The set for *Murder on the 2nd Floor* had been erected for the dress rehearsal. All was ready, until the Director wanted to know 'Where the b—– hell is the service lift?' – Apparently in the third act someone has to find a body in it! The author and publisher had omitted to mention it in the scenic inventory, the producer/director hadn't mentioned it at the production meeting, and Harold hadn't read the play at all! Consequently, there was a mad rush to get that lift constructed and the hammers were still being used as the first night audience were filing into the theatre.

Get your production secretary to arrange an early meeting with all concerned, the Stage Manager (or S.M.) and his full staff (or A.S.M.s). At this preliminary meeting, you should outline briefly your ideas about the theory of your interpretation, the convention and style of your production. Both will certainly affect the whole presentation of the show. They need to know your ideas about staging the production, this of course all depends on your findings when taking stock. (See Chapter Two).

You should certainly have a 'ground plan' of the shape of the staging you require, and be able to explain whether you need a box set, curtain or 'screen' settings, 'detail pieces' by the use of self-supporting flats, or a mere impression of theatrical fantasy. Theatrical licence or sheer impracticality may determine the setting. Many scripts (printed acting editions) have a ground plan of a set shown at the rear of the book. In most instances it is best to ignore these completely. They are either copies of the plans for the original professional production, or they are imaginative products of a staff member of the publisher. In both these instances, obviously no-one is aware of the situation and conditions in which *you* are going to work. If you are fortunate enough to have a stage designer in your midst, he or she will most probably have ideas and suggestions to offer. You will usually find that an experienced backstage staff will be very keen to contribute to the discussions, and so they should, but be aware of danger signals! Such enthusiasts will often have very ambitious ideas which may prove impractical, or may take so long to construct that other problems occur later . . . But do listen: they often come up with an idea that will solve problems that have been worrying you.

Here is a 'ground plan' for the 'Imaginary Play' I used as an example in Chapter Four. It shows you the size and structure of the set, the area S.L. and S.R. where, by bringing the fireplace and the door frame forward, it is possible to have gaps which give good viewing and access areas for the backstage staff. The setting area I have used is 22 feet wide, 14 feet in depth, with the width at the back reducing to 18 feet. Since the play is supposed to be set in a mansion, the doors, fireplace and so on are wider than in a normal house; the furniture, too, is more suited to its surroundings. The distance between the setting line and the proscenium arch is sufficient to allow the Stage Manager a view of the proceedings and to cope with the controls of the inter-communication system to dressing room and control box. That's if you're lucky enough to have such a luxury.

This example would no doubt be open to criticism at the initial meeting with the technicians, but at least you, as the Director, have given them a starting point for discussion.

However, after healthy argument, and armed with sufficient knowledge, a suitable design will be established and all must be aware of the final decision, for it affects all activities. If it is possible for a model to be constructed by a nimble-fingered member of the group, this can be referred to by everyone; the lighting team, who will be able to assess angles and levels, the sound engineers who will need to locate their speakers in appropriate positions; and the prop team, who will often have to manoeuvre large articles between flats, etc. The latter team will also want to know what area they have to furnish, whether in realistic or theatrical terms. If the model is painted in its stage colours, that, too, will be an important aid when they have to decide on the shades required in the supply of these articles.

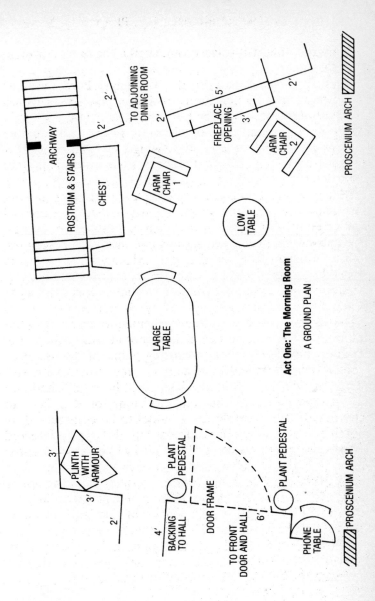

Act One: The Morning Room

A GROUND PLAN

The wardrobe staff will find the model a help for they can see at a glance if there are going to be any awkward doors or stairs for the cast to negotiate. If the cast is required to wear period or fantasy costumes, this will be a consideration for the designer.

Last but not least, the cast, who can accept more readily the architectural shape of the area in which they, as characters, move. All should be encouraged to study the plans and the model, and to make careful copies so that later dissension is avoided. The position of rostra, steps, doors, windows, and the setting of furniture, etc. should also be considered, even though later revision of these may occur, and if so, all should be informed, which is another task for the production secretary.

In the designing of the set, the position for the *prompt* needs to be considered. He or she must be out of sight of the audience, and within sight of the cast. So often no-one thinks of this, and the prompt is tucked away in the most inconvenient spot, out of sight *and earshot* and likely to finish up with bad eyes, frozen stiff, suffering from cramp and frustration. I have seen the *prompt* placed in the centre of the front row of seats, but it is not a practice of which I approve.

Stage Lighting

Once the design is agreed, the discussion should continue with the lighting of the set. This plan will all depend on the demands of the script, the lighting equipment available, and the possibility of being able to hire extra lamps, etc., if required. A check must also be made to ensure that the board and the supply of power to the building will allow such additions to be accommodated. This is a technical issue not within the terms of this book, but a competent electrician could advise on this subject.

The following facts should be understood:

a. You, as Director, will have to approve of the lighting plan that will be designed by the team.
b. You will be informed of any adjustments to that design.
c. Someone from the team will attend rehearsals at least some of the time, in order to become familiar with the importance of certain areas, the timing of lighting changes and technical effects.
d. Lighting plots and plans are ready *before* the technical rehearsals.
e. Once the team has set the final cues and the levels, they check precise co-ordination with the S.M.

Sound Effects

The people responsible for handling all sound effects should adopt a similar approach to that of the lighting team. Certainly their attendance at rehearsals is vital, particularly if the script calls for a great number of effects. Timing is important to a player desperately waiting for a cue. In a realistic convention the period and locale of the play must be studied for the authentic sound: e.g. an American telephone of the 1920s has a different ring from an English one; a telephone of the 1920s does not sound like one used in the 1960s. The slam of a heavy Elizabethan door sounds completely different from that of a modern one. A clock striking in a little country town doesn't sound like Big Ben, and it really is dreadful when a door bell rings off S.L. and the maid goes off to the hall at S.R. to answer it!

Music to create a receptive mood amongst the audience prior to a production is a great asset, particularly in an untheatrical atmosphere like a village hall or school. Music, or sounds (such as the throb of a drum, a beating heart, the ticking of a clock, or the howl of the wind) can be used to cover scene changes and continue the mood the director is seeking. Even music used during the intervals should continue the theme. I have known the atmosphere of an Edwardian style production, which was achieved so carefully, to be completely ruined by the loud amplification of a Glen Miller record played during the interval.

The Director should be aware of the importance of details such as this, and the S.M. needs to clarify (as with lighting) the effects plot both prior to and after the technical rehearsal.

Property Staff

These company members are responsible for furnishing the stage with everything that is of use to, or is used by, the players during the performance, and that includes:

- a. What they walk on: carpet, stage cloth, etc.
- b. What they sit on, or at: all furniture, exterior as well as interior.
- c. What they look at: general decor – but not the painting of the scenery.
- d. What they use: personal props, etc.
- e. What they eat or drink.

'Props' need to be aware of the style, convention and period of the production and their research into such details is vital.

The acting editions (already referred to) will give comprehensive lists, but often the Director will say that many of these items are superfluous to, or short of, the requirements for that particular production.

Thus it is important that 'props' attend all rehearsals, make notes of what is *actually required*, and what can be adjusted according to availability. Lists should be made and discussed with the S.M. When props are to be hired or borrowed, substitutes can be made for rehearsal purposes, and *should* be available immediately after the script has been 'blocked out' for movements of the players.

The lists should specify the nature of the props, from where they were acquired, and when they should be returned. A separate list is required to specify where and when they should be *set* on stage, and when and where they should be *struck* off stage.

Personal props, such as letters, guns, purses, etc should be listed and placed on the props table for the player who needs them, and checks should be made to ensure that the cast doesn't go on stage without them. It is also wise to make a special note of any valuables, and to ensure that such articles are placed in security after each performance. All personal items should be returned by players to the 'props' table.

The S.M. will also check progress on the construction and supply of props, and will require copies of all lists.

Wardrobe

This is another aspect of your production which requires special qualities, dedication, enthusiasm and adaptability. Even if the script to be tackled only requires the cast to wear modern dress, this should be co-ordinated – not only for colour, style, condition and quality, but for the credibility of the character and the locale. Too often players wear what *they* like, what suits *them*, irrespective of the situation, age, financial and class status of the character. During a performance of one of my plays *A Gathering of Doves* several of the women entered, all looking fairly tidy and smart, make-up fresh, hair immaculate, clothes uncreased. Yet according to the script it was early dawn and the characters had been up all night on the barricades of a riot-torn neighbourhood, where stones and petrol bombs had been thrown and people killed! When I remonstrated, one woman said: 'I always have my hair done on a Friday.' Words failed me!

Again, a Director should be consulted and given the opportunity to approve. If costumes are to be made, then designs and colours should be planned, the items listed so that colours don't clash (unless this is a deliberate choice) and that a pleasing combination is achieved. A professional costume designer will gather swatches of material in order to arrive at a certain quality of texture and colour. This is one aspect which is often forgotten in the amateur theatre.

Clothes for the players should be available for the first dress rehearsal at the latest so that checks can be made for fitting and suitability. Hired costumes need to be checked on arrival for condition, sizes, and to ensure that *all* have arrived. Often they are in a poor condition, and in this case, the company concerned should be contacted at once in an effort to get replacements. A good wardrobe staff will check that equipment is available for the care of clothes prior to, during, and after, the run of the show.

The Stage Manager

Time spent by the Director in personal and private discussion with the S.M. is always worthwhile. The S.M. can then assess the task he or she is facing on the technical issues of the production. This affords them prior information of your knowledge and attitudes as Director, and an opportunity to decide how many assistants will be required, and what part these assistants will play. For example, who will build the set or collate it from stock; who will attend to the scenic painting; who will form the property staff, and who is most suitable to deal with the problem of the scenic changes. In this instance they need to be strong, agile and quiet. All people backstage should wear dark clothes and soft-soled shoes; this is something upon which I insist.

It is also advisable to ensure that someone behind the scenes is responsible for fire precautions and general safety, ensuring that the company do not smoke on stage or in any vulnerable areas. If they are allowed to smoke in the dressing rooms, then care must be taken with the provision of ashtrays, and sand-filled dispensers. Many an outbreak of fire has been caused by a player rushing on stage and leaving a half-burnt cigarette leaning precariously in the dressing room. A constant check will avoid the danger.

The S.M. will also appoint one of their staff the Prompt, and I would ensure that this is *one* person, not a succession of 'odd bods' who have nothing to do at the time. A prompt needs dedication, patience, tact, a clear well-modulated vocal tone and quick reactions in an emergency.

Constant attendance at rehearsal is vital. From the outset, the prompt should mark in the script where pauses occur, and their length, particularly if a time count is specified. Normally a stroke thus / is enough to illustrate the short pause; double it // for a longer, or /^{5}/ for a time count. These may be altered as rehearsals proceed, so the use of a pencil is essential. Clear annotations on the script are so important and can certainly help to avoid any arguments.

While following the script carefully and constantly, a wise prompt will take the opportunity to study the players; they all have their idiosyncracies, and experience alone will enable these to be understood. There are those who welcome the assistance of the prompt, those who resent it, those who will always 'dry' at certain passages of the script, those who need the full line, those who are quick enough to take the brief cue. It is also important that the player's attention is directed to the line that has been paraphrased, though it is often better not to do this until after the rehearsal, or during some convenient break.

The task of a prompt is far from menial, and wise is the Director who can use this service with appreciation.

It is also the responsibility of the S.M. to ensure that your requirements are fulfilled, and *within the date* set at that initial technical meeting. Any problems that need your intervention or interest can be brought to your notice via the Production Secretary, who will by now be aware of the most appropriate and convenient time to interrupt you in *your* task: after all, you too have idiosyncracies that will affect relationships!

It should be understood by all that the S.M. is ultimately responsible for the 'running' of the show and once proceedings begin, must have the right to question the work in hand and its progress, and to impose his or her authority, where necessary, on all the stage staff and technicians. Ideally the S.M. should attend and be responsible for setting the room or stage, prior to rehearsals, with chalk lines (where possible) to represent the acting area, to provide rostra and furniture to represent that which will be used in performance, to strike these, if necessary, after rehearsal, and for the calling of all the cast for rehearsal. I am aware that only too often the S.M. is also heavily engaged in set construction, etc., but a well-informed S.M., as enthusiastic as the Director, will help to give a professional edge to any production, and the importance of a good Stage Manager is often not given sufficient recognition.

It is the S.M.'s knowledge of the details that helps him or her to create 'The Book', often called the 'Prompt Book', but not to be confused with the script used by the Prompt! An interleaved script of the play can often be obtained from the publishers, but, failing this, one breaks down the script from its binding and, using identically sized sheets of plain paper, interleaves the printed pages, punching the appropriate holes so that the entire script can be contained in a ring binder. It is worthwhile protecting the sheets with reinforcement rings (self-adhesive), otherwise constant use will damage the script. The interleaved sheets are then used to mark cues for lights, sounds, timing of the scenes, timing of tabs, cast calls, etc. All notes should again be made in pencil till they are confirmed at technical and final dress rehearsal.

Study of the sample 'Prompt Book' (see overleaf) will show that the S.M. also makes notes of the blocking of the basic moves. This enables them to take rehearsals if you are absent. In the professional theatre they are often called upon to take rehearsals of the understudies.

This typical 'Book' of the show demonstrates how, at a glance, the S.M. is able to check minute details that coordinate with the script.

I would advise any Director to prepare a similar Book before beginning rehearsals. It does enable one to make notes easily without cluttering up the script, to make notes about the blocking (the moves of the cast), the timing of the cues for the technical presentation, and it allows for

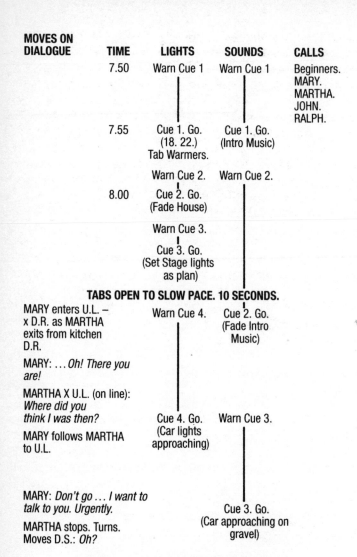

MOVES ON DIALOGUE	TIME	LIGHTS	SOUNDS	CALLS
	7.50	Warn Cue 1	Warn Cue 1	Beginners. MARY. MARTHA. JOHN. RALPH.
	7.55	Cue 1. Go. (18. 22.) Tab Warmers.	Cue 1. Go. (Intro Music)	
		Warn Cue 2.	Warn Cue 2.	
	8.00	Cue 2. Go. (Fade House)		
		Warn Cue 3.		
		Cue 3. Go. (Set Stage lights as plan)		

TABS OPEN TO SLOW PACE. 10 SECONDS.

MARY enters U.L. – x D.R. as MARTHA exits from kitchen D.R.		Warn Cue 4.	Cue 2. Go. (Fade Intro Music)	
MARY: ...*Oh! There you are!*				
MARTHA X U.L. (on line): *Where did you think I was then?*		Cue 4. Go. (Car lights approaching)	Warn Cue 3.	
MARY follows MARTHA to U.L.				
MARY: *Don't go ... I want to talk to you. Urgently.*			Cue 3. Go. (Car approaching on gravel)	
MARTHA stops. Turns. Moves D.S.: *Oh?*				

EXAMPLE PAGE FROM PROMPT (S.M.) BOOK

easy coordination with the S.M. At the conclusion of rehearsals the two Books should bear identical basics, though obviously personal notes may differ.

I appreciate the fact that the Director will be eager to start working on the text of the production, but I can assure you that the preparations I have written about in these early chapters are extremely valuable and are, in fact, part of the creative process. Such practical points serve several purposes, giving the whole proceedings a business-like impression to all, helping to establish a confidence which will be echoed throughout rehearsals. Only a genius can work 'in limbo' and there are but a few of those around, especially in the amateur field.

The success of *your* production depends on the people who contribute so much of their time and skills. They are often unsung and unheralded. But if they are confident of your requirements, you'd be wise to leave them to get on with it, while you have another look at the script. The first task is to get the thing moving, and to organise a rehearsal schedule.

Chapter Seven

THE PLANNING OF REHEARSALS

It is your task as Director to mould performances into the framework of your interpretation, but the players' contribution of talent mustn't be rejected, only adapted, and that is where the organisation of rehearsals and economical use of the time available is so important.

With all the factors before you, you should now be able to plan the process. Don't call players to rehearsal unless they are going to be used either in scenes you are directing, in a word-rehearsal with your production secretary who will be keeping a watchful eye and ear for any deviations of script or interpretation, or unless they are required for wardrobe fitting, etc. However, do insist on prompt and required attendance, and early notification of their inability to attend due to some emergency. It is sheer bad manners on their part not to do this and you need to state your attitude firmly but tactfully.

All dramatic groups have their own ideas about the length of rehearsals and whether they stop for refreshments or not. I have strong views on the subject and will not stop, for the momentum once lost is hard to regain, and much time is wasted. It is better to work hard and profitably for a couple of hours or so, and then relax and perhaps discuss what has been developed or discovered during the rehearsal.

In the professional theatre, obviously the hours spent in rehearsal are long, but the weeks spent are few, and it is the full-time occupation of the company. In the amateur world, all have finished a hard day's work, and in my opinion it is useless rehearsing to very late in the evening: everyone is tired, exhausted, and because little progress is made, people begin to get tetchy and irritable. Short, sharp rehearsals are usually the most rewarding of all.

When you have made your plans, ensure that all concerned (and that includes technical staff), are aware of the schedule, which is another task for the production secretary.

Every Director has an individual style of working, but basically the following procedure is a sensible one which allows you to see progress and development:

1. The basic framework. Blocking, Movement and Motivation.
2. Development of Character and Character relationships.
3. Development of Purpose. The Conflicts, Contrasts and Climax of the Plot.

At this point it's a good idea to leave time for reflection. Are the developments on the right lines? Are the cast growing into their characters, giving depth and vocal variety? Is that 'business' slick enough? No doubt you are aware of the few weaknesses in the chain, the links, the 'pieces' of that jigsaw. Don't be tempted to ignore the defects: it will be too late if you don't correct them now.

In checking these points, it is often better to try and fit in a few private rehearsals where you can really get to grips with the problem. Sometimes it is a help to drop the scripts and improvise. For example, I was directing a play set in a small Hungarian village. Nearly all the able-bodied men had gone off to war, leaving the women hungry, irritable and frustrated. A stranger comes to the area; he is strong, vibrant, the tension rises as some of the women seek his favours. Technically all seemed well, yet the animal quality I was seeking was missing, so I suggested an improvisation of a scene in the jungle – each character reflected by the relevant animal: the talkative gossip was a small monkey; the quiet, sulky one a snake; the strong dominating one a lioness, and so on. Through growth of understanding of the motives and movements of the animals as they sought their prey, they began to express the qualities I was seeking. They became sinuous, quick to pounce, artful and fierce.

Time must also be given to the technical staff to check their contribution to the production. I know that later technical rehearsals are held in full, but it does save a great deal of hassle if they can test out that tricky problem of technical business prior to those occasions. Certainly by now they should be aware of when and where it occurs, but an actual practice at this point will enable them to remedy any weakness and polish their techniques, just as the players are doing.

This respite will give other people an opportunity to talk to you, or the wardrobe or props department. They are bound to have queries they don't want to leave till the last minute, and you are the only person who can make the final decision. Here is another opportunity for the production secretary actively to assist, by taking some of the players through those weak passages, where the command of dialogue isn't complete, where the timing of business wants checking. No time is wasted.

When planning rehearsals for a production that involves music, singing and dancing, the process must, by the nature of the genre, be altered. The pieces of the jigsaw are different from those of a straight play. The choreography of dance must be rehearsed separately; the Musical Director will need to ensure that the principals and soloists conform to his interpretation of the music, and it isn't till all the cast are familiar with those aspects of the production that you can really get down to the 'floor' work of the show, the blocking and the general pattern of movement.

Therefore, co-operation is essential to ensure that maximum use is made of time and talent, while still keeping a large company interested in the project. While dance and song rehearsals are in progress, with careful planning you should still be able to fix some times when you take the principals through the libretto and the developments of the characters and plot.

Once you commence the putting together of the sections, the process of normal stage directional practices apply, especially bearing in mind my previous advice about avoiding a 'Rent a Crowd' look about the chorus.

I mentioned in an earlier chapter that I am often asked how long should rehearsals take for an amateur production. It is very difficult to answer that question, because there can be no hard and fast rule. I do feel that there is a tendency for groups to rehearse for too long a period, but not hard enough – though there are exceptions.

It all depends on the company, their dedication, the script they are tackling, and the Director. I would suggest that a rehearsal period of eight weeks should be adequate for a straight, three-act play: two rehearsals weekly for the first four weeks, with extra calls as the production date approaches.

So, after the re-assessment and the checking, a renewal of energy should bring you into those final stages of polishing, tightening of cues, the checking of the tempo, speech variation and audibility, the credibility of performances, and right into the Technical Rehearsals and the Dress Rehearsal.

Chapter Eight

BLOCKING

Throughout this book I have laid stress on the importance of familiarity with the script; with the author's intention; with the convention and style required in presentation and performance. At no stage is this more important than now, when you need to confirm your interpretation with action.

Theatre is as much visual as oral, and the manner in which the characters move and are grouped will add strength to your conviction of their purpose. Whether they are motivated by changing moods and emotions, realistic practicality or sheer theatrical spectacle, there needs to be a design about their traversing of the stage, their entrances and their exits.

Thus time must be spent prior to the preliminary rehearsals to consider this vital task. 'Acting editions' of the script will include details like 'Mary crosses S.L. to the sideboard.'

This is all very well, but do remember my previous warning. Like the ground plans included in these editions, these moves are based on the original production, or come from some fragment of imagination of the publisher's staff. They would not refer to *your* staging, *your* conception of the script at all. I would advise all Directors to ignore such

61

instructions, delete them from the script and memory. The only exceptions, perhaps, being the instructions about the time of entrances and exits of the characters, but even then, delete the 'where' unless applicable.

The players, as characters, need to know their places in the world of the play, and it isn't sufficient to say 'You come in D.R. cross U.S.L. and sit in Armchair I'. That's a direct move, and rather a long way to go in one move: it will look odd, the player will not be happy; but if you say (and only if it's true) 'Come in from the Hall D.R. and move to that armchair U.L. because you're making a claim to it, before anyone else gets there', both the audience and the player will see the point and respect the truth.

It will look false if you direct: 'You're masking Jane, so break up to the fireplace and get out of her way' but if you question: 'Doesn't Jane's nearness make you feel cold? Right, get closer to the fire', then it becomes a natural reaction, the motivation is there and it underlines the attitude of one character to another.

Some Directors tend to leave the cast to move around the stage area as they wish, only suggesting an alteration when obviously necessary. Certainly the cast need to be familiar with the locale and the setting of the play, but several problems tend to arise with that method. No-one knows exactly where the others are going to be at a particular moment, for players are fickle and tend to change their minds from performance to performance. A visual muddle is often apparent, and an experienced, albeit selfish, player would hog the acting area to the detriment of the natural flow of movement. And, of course, they eventually up-stage everyone else in the play.

Other Directors tend to be very rigid about the blocking of a script, ensuring that the cast are regimented to the nth degree, never deviating from one foot to another.

Since directing is a creative art, I feel that a certain amount of flexibility is essential; you know the pattern you are seeking, but the players, too, should at least have the opportunity to express the character they are trying to create. It is better to give them a basic framework of moves to begin with and see what happens as rehearsals develop.

In Chapter Four, I referred to the 'jigsaw' approach. Now is the time to study again the pieces, the sections of the script. Some are more important than others, some more complex; the rest are the links that join them together. While a degree of continuity becomes necessary as rehearsals progress, don't get tied down in a 'we must get through this act tonight' syndrome. It is a failing that tends to weaken many amateur productions. Better to tackle shorter, difficult sections, concentrate on them to get them right, rather than to dissipate time, energy and, what is more important, that creative adrenalin which requires feeding with enthusiasm. Once these sections are correct, they can be slotted into the links and the chain of continuity is complete.

Since much must be retained in the memory (for a competent Director cannot study the script too closely *and* watch the cast) I would advise that blocking should be undertaken in small stages, i.e. a few sections at a time. Ideally, you need to block out, and at the *same rehearsal* give the cast a re-run to confirm those basic moves. The players have much to assimilate, and giving them too many directions, without a chance for them to make the essential notes in their scripts, and an opportunity to confirm those moves by a practical movement run, is expecting too much.

While on the subject of notes, it is an asset if *all concerned* (and that goes for you as well) use a simple formula of stage terms when making notes in scripts. If, in an emergency, an understudy has to be called upon, it is hopeless if they are given a script which looks as if a child has been scribbling away like mad, or even an adult graffiti artist. Weird and wonderful are the notes I have seen in my time. Some of them would have put Salvador Dali to shame!

Stage shorthand is simple and easily identifiable. Thus the stage acting area positions:

BACK OF STAGE

UR		UC		UL
	URC		ULC	
R	RC	C	LC	L
	DRC		DLC	
DR		DC		DL

FRONT OF STAGE

U = Up stage, i.e. *away from the audience.*
D = Down stage, i.e. *towards the audience.*
C = Centre stage.
R = Right.
L = Left.
X = Crosses from one position to another.
С = Turns.
∧ = Tempo increasing.
∨ = Tempo decreasing.

Insist that all moves are noted in pencil, since changes will take place as the rehearsals progress. Where stage 'business' is concerned, special attention must be given to the timing and the process, e.g.:

When the custard pie is being taken on to stage, at what point it is thrown, and the precise moment when the expected recipient ducks.

64

Another tip to aid your memory, is to prepare your plan of blocking as near as possible to the actual rehearsal. It helps you to retain the visual aspect of that scene, the reasons why you have created that aspect. Let's use my imaginary play as an example . . .

1. It was important at that particular point in the dialogue that John appeared to be dominant, by his position on the staircase U.S.L., while Martha and Mary were grouped below him – the former D.R. of the C. table, the latter S.L. of the coffee table.
2. It was essential that Martha was hidden by the open door at S.R. while John and Mary were talking D.L.C.
3. It was while Jane was on the phone D.R. facing the audience, that Mary was able to creep down the stairs and exit S.L. without being seen.
4. It made for a stronger impact to have Ralph, the employer, standing U.R. (the sunlight shining upon his face) while the rest of the cast are grouped L. Jane in armchair I, John standing U.S. of her chair, Martha in armchair 2. D.L.

   His isolation set him apart from his staff, the police sergeant has a larger area in which he can move freely, adjusting his position to the individual, or to the dramatic content of his questions, and when the final dénouement comes, the focus changes dramatically from S.L. to U.R. It makes easy access to C. stage as Ralph comes down to face his accusers.

So, with the model of the set close to hand, gradually go through that initial introductory scene and move and adjust the characters according to their purpose in your interpretation of the author's intention.

The inexperienced Director may find it a help to use

coloured counters to represent each character, and move them about in an effort to get the required effect. Another tip is to draw a small sketch of the set at crucial parts of the script with the initial letter of the character (or a similar symbol) to represent the characters and their position at that point.

Do remember that at this stage you are only planning the outline of movement. In many instances, e.g. when long speeches are involved, it is better to declare an 'open area' and see how the player uses it to interpret the characters in movement; then this can be polished and confirmed in later rehearsals.

Your copy of the 'prompt book' should contain only those essential moves and grouping, the detail can be filled in later. So again to our 'imaginary play', and this example of the Director's Book.

EXAMPLE OF DIRECTOR'S BLOCKING IN PROMPTBOOK

Dialogue	*Moves*
(1) MARY enters from top of stairs. Goes towards hall door as MARTHA appears. (2)	(1) MARY at U.L. x D.R.
	(2) MARTHA at D.R.
(3) MARTHA: *Where did you think I was?*	(3) MARTHA x U.L.
(4) MARY: *Don't go . . . I want to talk to you.*	(4) MARY x U.L.C. Stops.
(5) MARTHA: (belligerently) Oh! (The lights of an approaching car are seen)	(5) MARTHA stops.

(6) MARY: Quick . . . *Before*   (6) MARY quickly to
    the master comes. I've got   D.S. of MARTHA.
    something to ask you.

This is a very simple example of the process. The dialogue is of course already printed in the script, and the moves noted in the plain interleaving of the Director's script. You will see that in some situations it is helpful to note *exactly* where one character stands in relation to another – as in Move (6) when Mary moves quickly to Martha but stands not to her side, or 'above' her (i.e. upstage of her) but downstage of her.

There are six basic moves shown, and they each help to create immediately an air of tension, one character on the attack, one stalling, their relationship clearly defined. You will note that the dialogue that is spoken, *as the move is made*, is italicised. The cue number of the move 1–5, (written against the dialogue side of the script), is noted at the beginning of the line. If a move is made halfway through a line, then it is marked at the point where the move should begin, and the line stops when the move is to cease (note move 5).

In all moves, there must be motivation, even if it appears to be obscure. Remember, the players will be happier if you help them to understand their objectives.

From the players' point of view there are two basic moves, conscious and unconscious. The first is triggered by purpose, the second is a response, a reflex.

e.g. a. conscious movement: the deliberate move to a chair
                               to sit.

    b. unconscious movement: the automatic reflex of a
                         hand as it touches some-
                         thing that feels repulsive.

The audience will be aware both of movement that has
dramatic value, and movement that has none. This applies
equally to the theatrical convention, for a purely artistic
movement can be dramatically viable.

As a general rule it is understood that where *a movement*
is of dramatic significance, it should not be accompanied by
dialogue.

    e.g.: as the condemned man walks to the scaffold.

Whereas when *the dialogue* is of dramatic significance, it
should not be accompanied by movement.

    e.g.: as the condemned man makes his last speech before
        execution.

Of course there are exceptions, but as I said earlier, one
has to know the rules before they can be broken.

    Ensure that variation is introduced where possible, but
not without purpose.

I was once asked to give advice to a drama group at the
secondary stages of production. After about three weeks
rehearsal, I was surprised to see all the cast sitting round
the table repeating their lines. On commenting about this,
the 'director' said: 'Oh . . . I'm going to get that organised
tonight.' He started by suggesting where the cast should be
sitting or standing at the very outset. They did so, and then
proceeded with the dialogue for about five minutes or more,
the 'director' closely scrutinising his script to ensure that
they were speaking the right lines. Then he rose, and
stopped them by saying: 'Right . . . I think it's about here
we will give the audience a change of picture; and that he
proceeded to do, merely by making the cast swop positions

and chairs. Again I politely remonstrated, only to be told in a withering tone, 'I believe that the play is the thing', the play in this instance being written by the gentleman himself.

In the *theatrical convention* all kinds of movement are possible.

In the *realistic/naturalistic convention* truth must prevail, or at least, appear to.

In a production where *Style* is essential, a certain artificiality of movement is accepted. In a 'Comedy of Manners' behaviour is paramount.

Grouping: This is a problem which gives many a headache to inexperienced Directors, especially if they have a large cast working on a small stage. They will be perplexed over the problems of masking, and avoiding those straight lines which, as an adjudicator, I deplore, and which I see too often, particularly in musicals. Extras are lined up, looking in vain for a purpose or a place. They never seem to know where or who they are, or how they are to react in certain situations. Groupings of several players or large numbers should always be considered for the focal points, e.g. the predominating character, the opposing factor, the developing conflict or the contrast. These groupings need to be adjusted as the situations change from the weak to the strong, or the attacker versus the defender, etc.

What is so often overlooked is that in any crowd, everyone is an individual and, if you can give each extra an identity, how much more truthful is their contribution, and how much more satisfaction they will gain during performance!

For example, take Scene 2 ('the noble child') from Bertolt Brecht's *The Caucasian Chalk Circle*:

The locale is outside a palace gateway of an Eastern city, many years ago.

The Governor, his wife, his entire entourage (some of whom are plotting against him) are on their way to the church for the christening of the young Prince, the heir. The Governor is a harsh dictator; his wife selfish and greedy. Their régime is cruel; many poor people suffer. As the procession leaves the palace at S.R., it is followed by a crowd of citizens of the town, some bearing petitions, others asking for alms, for clemency, for food, for justice.

Technically, the Director has to make the crowd appear larger than it is; they have to try to get near the Governor, but they are repelled by his Blackshirts. Other peasants try to push in front. There is *relevant* dialogue from some members of the court as they traverse the stage and before they enter the church, which is at S.L. Quite a problem.

It is therefore wise to ensure that the clothing worn by the extras is nondescript and quickly interchangeable. Give them all an identity and a purpose. A wronged merchant and his wife; a petty thief; a deserted wife with two starving children; a blind man; a crippled girl; two conspirators who seek revenge for some wrong; homeless vagrants; a dying woman; a political agitator, etc. Some can be grouped around the church with a few whose bodies are visible but not their faces, and as the procession approaches the church, they can mingle with the extras who have moved forward from S.R. They can create further diversion at the rear. In this way, the crowd appears larger than it is and, with careful timing of the surge forward and the repelling by the soldiers, the few relevant lines of dialogue can be slotted in over the apparent melée.

Amongst the crowd, appoint a few 'leaders' who can stir up their particular group at a given point. The whole pattern of movement will need choreographing, but the end result is a vast improvement on two straight lines looking like commuters waiting for a train.

In such scenes with extras, it isn't necessary for everyone's face to be seen. What is essential is to give the impression of lively 'involved' onlookers. Some may be involved with a neighbour, therefore in profile to the audience, some sitting, some standing on a variety of levels.

The same principle can apply even to a small cast. A side view of a player can reveal as much of that character as a view of the face, and a sharp turn of a back can punctuate a line of dialogue very effectively.

Contrasts are often strengthened by the 'triangle'. The protagonist is the apex, then, as the balance of argument changes, so does the grouping; but all moves must appear truthful, otherwise they look planned.

There are bound to be many occasions when a planned move seems effective to you during your pre-rehearsal blocking, but looks far from right when the player takes the direction and moves into the position as asked.

You must query, is it that the player is not following your line of thought, or that he or she doesn't accept the motivation of the character at that point? It is futile to carry on hoping that it will come naturally as rehearsals proceed. A halt must come when you either try to explain why that move is important to you, or get the cast to move as *they* feel is right. Sometimes you are wrong, because of the natural emotion the playing of the character is creating within an actor.

It is always advisable at this stage to consider the curtain call and to ensure when working on the finale of the show that all are aware of your intentions. Far too often this is left to the dress rehearsal, and, since it's the last the audience sees of your cast, I feel it is very important to keep up the good impression you hope to have made during the show! It may be that you wish to make a 'specialised' picture, a tableau, or the normal line-up. Whatever it is, it must be rehearsed to be as slick as any other section; the manner in which the cast enter on the stage, how they are positioned, and the timing of their bow/curtsey to the audience – like guardsmen rather than lilies waving on the wind!

Once the process of blocking is complete, you must press on with the next stages. Your cast should have been given a date for abandoning their books, for being completely familiar with the dialogue. Players are still themselves with a script in their hands. They cannot act or react with their eyes on the lines, the prompt is there, and if they are doing their job properly, their contribution will be an asset to all.

Chapter Nine

JOHN BROWN'S BODY

By the time the action has been blocked out, the players should certainly be aware of the innate nature of the characters they are portraying; and yet how often do we see a player (say by the name of John Brown) appearing in show after show for the local dramatic group, in a variety of rôles, yet, apart from a change of dialogue and clothes, always seeming to be no different? His stance, his gestures, speech patterns and mannerisms are always the same, because he is still, in essence, playing John Brown!

In some instances, this applies to the professional theatre. There are certain players who are always 'typed', and who make their name giving the one performance, but it is not a policy to pursue in the normal circumstances of theatre.

Acting is an art form, its techniques acquired through a great deal of study and experience. Some people are more talented than others, and have a natural aptitude for the theatre. Very fortunate are the directors who have such people at their disposal.

Obviously, in the professional theatre, where the actors are to a large extent under the control of their trade union Equity, the players who attend auditions are fully trained and the work of the Director is less onerous as a result. This benefit allows for greater flexibility of mind and material in interpretation and productioon.

In the amateur theatre, the Director has invariably not only to direct the show, but has also, in passing, to teach the cast something about the art of performing. The true representation of the characters in the situation is vital, otherwise the production becomes a pale shadow of the author's intention. As Director you must, as rehearsals proceed, guide, cajole, and encourage your cast to use their attributes in creating that fundamental truth.

Take movement, for example. We all have a psychological pattern of movement. This is something which is our very own, as individual as our fingerprints.

Study a selection of people, moving about in a variety of ways:–

a. A housewife: washing up, making beds, cleaning, doing all the tasks involved with housekeeping.
b. A typist in an office: taking letters, filing, answering the 'phone, eating luncheon sandwiches, etc.
c. A road mender, a construction worker, a shop assistant, etc.

You will note that they all go about their tasks, even sitting down or walking about, in a different manner from someone else doing the same thing: it's a 'pattern of movement' which is individual to *them*.

The pattern affects us all in three ways, and all players should make a self study of their own 'pattern' and be aware of it.

1. *Movement in space.* This is literally what it says – the amount of room we inhabit when we walk about, sit

down, tackle any given task. It applies not only to width, but to length as well, e.g. small steps as opposed to large strides.

Some people are very neat, contained in their movements, and their approach disturbs little of their surroundings or their neighbours.

In contrast, other people are greedy in their use of space, they tend to flail their arms about as they walk, throw their clothes about, sprawl untidily in a chair, spread the dirty dishes over every surface, and they are not necessarily large people.

2. *Movement in time.* Again, self-explanatory. It tells of the speed at which we move; but fast movements do not mean that we accomplish more, complete a task quicker or more efficiently than a slower rival. A good example of this was illustrated by Aesop in his fable of 'The Hare and the Tortoise'.

3. *Movement in Dynamic Terms.* In other words, the amount of energy we unleash in general action: e.g. some people shake hands forcibly, others limply; some people can be heard approaching from some way off and they pound along the floor, others can be directly behind you before you are aware of their presence.

All these elements need to be studied in making a judgment on the character to be portrayed.

Again we need to study the manner and movement in terms of the physical habits which our joints adopt over a period of time. These are affected by our bone structure, our health, our environment, our age, our profession, etc. For example:

A ballet dancer who will invariably adopt a stance in the third position.
A soldier who becomes military in bearing and tread.
A miner who, because it is often the position in which he works, will squat when relaxing.

We are also affected by what we are wearing (a) on our heads, (b) around our bodies, and (c) on our feet.

The manner of approach varies. There are many famous players who can assess the movement of a character through ensuring they have the right shoes, and it's certainly an approach with which I have much sympathy. Consider the difference in the tread when wearing varying heights of heels, Wellington boots, soft slippers or walking barefoot. Peter Barkworth tells (in his book *About Acting*) how Wendy Hiller, on being offered the rôle of the late Queen Mary in the play *Crown Matrimonial* by Royce Royton, thought a while, then proceeded to walk about the room. After a while she smiled. She had been carefully adjusting her movements, and said: 'Those feet are royal. I can build on that.' And she did, very successfully.

Consider the trunk. How different a woman will feel when she is wearing a long skirt with many petticoats, or a corset, or a crinoline.

Similarly, both stance and movement are affected by a head scarf, an old béret, a top hat, or an Edwardian hat with a long feather boa draped round the shoulders.

A wise Director will encourage the wearing of suitable substitutes as early in rehearsal as possible, and should help the cast in their attempts to present the truth.

In making a character study, it is also essential that all players are aware of the *situation* and *circumstances* that affect movement. A Director must be able to watch and know if the characters are being realistic as they walk about the stage. Do remember that if the *theatrical* convention is being followed the approach may differ. Further study will show that some people walk from their hips, which creates a sinuous movement usually associated with people who are familiar with walking barefoot, or who have a natural rhythmic glide. Other people walk from their knees, keeping their hips taut, which tends to make for abrupt, jerky movements.

So, while the cast should by now know their own personal style of movement, they have to think about adjusting it to suit the character, and much detail must be considered. For example, in playing an elderly person, there are those who think it is sufficient to bend their backs and shuffle about the stage. This is a generalisation and doesn't necessarily apply. Many people remain alert and upright till the end of their days. You, as Director, must watch and correct if the false impression is given. As a general principle, what happens in old age is this: Muscles stretch and sag, they lose the elasticity of youth, the feet are harder to lift, the skin loses its freshness, breath comes in shorter contractions – but that doesn't necessarily mean having a bent back and displaying signs of senility.

The character is an individual, and shaped by individual circumstances. Readjusting the personal movement of a player takes time and study, but at least John Brown will appear to be a different character from his first entrance, before he even speaks.

Gestures and mannerisms are also aspects of performance that can help to illuminate a character, but they *must* be used with great care and discretion. For example,

(a) An odd scratch of the head can indicate a concentration on a train of thought. Repeated too often, and it only suggests an infestation of lice!

(b) A rubbing together of the hands is a cliché that is meant to suggest avarice. Overdone, it suggests an onset of hypothermia.

(c) A character who *may* be 'gay' doesn't have to 'camp' it up with the hand on the hips and the limp wrist: such things ruin the play and are more suitable to a 'drag act'.

One of the most effective gestures I have seen was that of an actress playing Louisa (one of the slightly mentally retarded sisters in *Ladies in Retirement*). She has a dislike of anything that represents Catholicism, and when another character offers her a pear that has come from the garden of a nearby convent, she refuses it curtly. It is pressed upon her, so she takes it, puts it down as quickly as possible, and then slowly wipes her fingers down the side of her dress with distaste. Just the one gesture, but it revealed so much.

So a Director must look for such action and reaction: sometimes to create or encourage it, sometimes to diffuse it, at other times to quell it completely because it is not in context.

Another tricky point to study is the *degree* or amount of action that must be taken in certain circumstances, where it is *secondary* to the main action of the moment, for instance when the continuation of stage 'business' is *complementary to* but not the activity itself, which your interpretation of the script wishes to underline at that moment. Consider the first half of the double bill *Celebration* by Willis Hall and Keith Waterhouse; it is called *The Wedding* and is set during one evening, in an upper room over a public house. When the curtain rises, the room is in a bit of a shambles. It is a room which is hired out for various activities, and all kind of rubbish is still stored there. It is neither clean nor inviting. During the play the family has to sweep it out, clear out the rubbish, set up three trestle tables, chairs, and decorate the room with bunting and coloured streamers, lay out cloths, cutlery, china, napkins, flowers, etc. in fact the whole setting for a wedding breakfast which will be served on the following day. While this is taking place, there is a constant stream of visitors, some helping, others hindering, some making arrangements for their transport to the church.

The main part of the play is the inter-relationships of the characters – the *practical* business described above is secondary. It is not until the wedding cake is taken out of its box and set on the centre table, that the audience are really aware of what has been going on, and when it is well done, they are taken aback and applaud enthusiastically. The secret is, of course, to choreograph the activities, drawing attention away from them to the main speakers of the time, and secondly, to ensure that the action isn't rushed, isn't noisy, but is handled smoothly and *on set cues*. Discipline and care in timing are all-important.

This applies equally to personal activities such as knitting, doing tapestry, pouring tea, etc. While the audience will respect the fact that the activity is part of the truth of the character or the situation, it needs to be tackled in relation to the demands of that situation.

Clicking knitting needles, the rattle of tea-cups, the rapid movement of an arm as a tapestry frame is encircled – all this can be distracting, but taken at *half* the normal speed it can still appear to be authentically done. Of course, in contrast, one may suddenly need to draw the attention of the audience to the 'business' and a reverse procedure, of loud noise or quick movements, will be effective if well-timed.

One particular point of weakness that I note at Festivals is the player who deems it necessary to stop all dialogue while a secondary action is being performed. That is only necessary when the *action itself* is all-important.

Stance is another aspect of movement that needs to be watched. It is also affected by the pattern of movement and other factors I have previously mentioned.

There is no need for constant movement, for a certain stillness can point some attitudes more effectively than a fidget, particularly if other characters are moving about. It's the contrast that underlines the character, and, of course, the reverse is also true.

One of the directions that is often given in a script is 'he *paces* up and down'. Now, if this is taken literally, it looks rather ridiculous. It is meant to suggest inner turmoil and agitation. In fact, such a mood is expressed more truthfully in the odd adjustment of position and stance, a movement of no more than a foot or so, perhaps interposed with a sudden move to a greater distance. It is the *truth* you are seeking, for *that* character in *that* situation.

One of the constant cries of an amateur player is, 'I don't know what to do with my hands!' As an adjudicator I am very much aware of this weakness, as I see players constantly opening their arms, from the elbows, with hands open in a 'Who will buy?' gesture. Or perhaps they are standing with their hands placed on the front of their skirts or trousers, looking not unlike a bunch of bananas. Arms and hands must be free to be flexible, so as to appear natural when a gesture of action or reaction is required.

The main reason for the fault is the stance adopted by the players. They are invariably standing with their shoulders dropped forward. This means that when the arms are moved they tend to be 'locked' at the elbow, which will then restrict movement. If the player stands erect, lifts the shoulders back, and allows the arms to hang easily by the sides, movement is relaxed and both hands and arms will be able to gesture with a more natural ease. Those embarrassing 'bananas' will be gone, and no one will be asking for customers.

Period stance and movement should be studied and mastered when essential to the production. Certain periods had their own Style and Manners. The way in which a curtsey or bow was given, and to whom. The handling of a fan, the fingering of a cravat, the taking of snuff. Stage fights, too, need to be precisely choreographed and rehearsed for split-second timing. Text books are available on all these subjects, and a Director needs to be aware of the correct procedure; if you are not an expert on such matters, seek help rather than ignore the problem.

As I said at the beginning of the chapter, there is so much that can be achieved by a player who is aware of what the body can do, how it can express so much before they even speak.

Think of the mannerisms of race, one has only to see the shrug of the shoulders constantly used, and one immediately thinks of the French, the wildly waving hands, and an Italian is conjured up, sombre inflexibility could suggest a Russian. All these points, not overdone but merely suggested, can speak volumes.

As rehearsals proceed and the characters develop, the astute Director needs to be aware of these factors. It's part of the job of the Director – even if by now you are thinking that you need eyes, ears and eyes in the back of your head – you're right, you do!

But on to the dialogue – so make sure your ears are attuned to the script.

Chapter Ten

'SPEAK THE SPEECH, I PRAY YOU . . .'
(*Hamlet* Act 3, scene 2)

It is obvious that William Shakespeare had good reason for penning the following lines for Hamlet, in his 'advice to the players':

Speak the speech, I pray you, as I pronounced it to you, trippingly on the tongue; but if you mouth it, as many of our players do, I had as lief the town crier spoke my lines . . .

Shakespeare was an actor who wrote for 'The King's Men', the company of which he was an active member for many years. He must have been aware of the manner in which a poor performance could ruin his lines. He even drew attention to the question of movement and gesture which I dealt with in the previous chapter, for Hamlet continues,

Nor do not saw the air too much with your hands, thus, but use all gently; for in the very torrent, tempest, and as I may say, whirlwind of your passion, you must acquire and beget a temperance that may give it smoothness.

83

And later:

> Suit the action to the word, the word with the action;
> with this special observance, that you o'er step not the
> modesty of nature . . .

All good advice to any player. In the convention of realism
this is imperative; even in the convention of theatricality,
where the characters are creations of fantasy, there must be
a relevant truth in that fantasy.

The delivery of the dialogue is the most important aspect
to be considered when taking rehearsals, as you attempt to
bring the writer's text to life. 'John Brown', again, must
delve further into the character he is portraying to discover
clues which will help him to interpret the lines with truth.

In speech, as in movement, we each have our own indi-
viduality:

1. IN VOLUME: and this does not necessarily mean that
   because a player is loudly spoken, he or she is any
   more audible than someone who has a softer tone.
2. IN CLARITY: where enunciation is precise, articu-
   lation pure, unimpeded by the slurring and swallowing
   of the words.
3. IN RATE: which is the *speed* of delivery of language.
4. IN PACE: which is the rate at which cues are 'picked
   up' and followed.
5. IN RESONANCE: which is the degree of a resounding
   tone colour or timbre.
6. IN PITCH: which is the level of musical sound depend-
   ing on the comparative rapidity of vibrations, i.e. the
   tendency for a male to 'pitch' his voice in the lower
   register, in comparison with the female whose 'pitch'
   is much higher.

7. VOCAL VARIATION: where the preceding qualities are brought into use to produce our own individual musical scale of speech.

Other factors which determine our speech patterns are:-

a. AGE: a thinner quality of sound is often produced as the vocal chords and throat muscles grow weaker.
b. RACE: which will affect a 'character' portrayal, since a variation of language will bring different stresses in vocal chords.
c. PHYSICAL CONDITION: Illness, shortness of breath or pain will create vocal problems.
d. MENTAL CONDITION: Emotional stress will bring differing variations of speech.
e. ENVIRONMENT: The family background, the locale of our upbringing, the speech pattern of those around us will be adopted at the beginning of speech. We copy these patterns in childhood, they are normal to us and they will stay with us unless a conscious effort is made to change them.
f. EDUCATION: when experience and training will make us aware of the value of clear communication.

Thus the speech patterns and vocal attributes of each player must be assessed and readjusted if the truth of the character is to be drawn.

e.g. If 'John Brown' is a precise, efficient, well-educated, sober, middle-aged business man with an 'Oxbridge' delivery of clear consonants and rounded vowels, he will have to make several adjustments if he is to portray Alfred Doolittle, the dustman in George Bernard Shaw's play *Pygmalion*.

It is not sufficient to direct: 'Doolittle is a Cockney dustman who likes a drink, so loosen the speech, flatten the vowels and drop a few aitches.'

Doolittle may be a Cockney dustman, but he has a natural rhetorical delivery, and is well able to express his philosophical yearnings. He has several long speeches in the play which certainly demonstrate his lack of grammatical knowledge, but any attempt to stem the flow with excessive laziness of speech would destroy the essence of the character.

There are always subtleties which can make or mar character idioms.

Directors must listen for audibility, but audibility matched with vocal variation. Projection will be attained through the 'throwing' of the voice from a forward position, ensuring that words are not swallowed. Mumbling of dialogue is to be avoided, unless it is required *as part of the purpose of the play*.

I would stress the importance of special emphasis on projection at the rise of the curtain (the main tabs), and at the first entrance of any player.

The acoustics of any building are fixed according to the design and the materials used in construction, but they will vary in certain circumstances.

They will be affected by:-

a. The weather, since it affects the absorbent qualities of some building materials and fabrics.
b. Exterior activities, aircraft, traffic, etc.
c. The size of the audience, since the amount of empty space in the building will affect the sound.

The main point to remember is that while waiting for the opening of the production, the audience will have become attuned to the noises around them, and to the acoustical qualities as they exist *at that particular moment*. There will be the chatter of human voices, the tread of feet, the banging of seats, House music, a rustle of programmes and so on.

Then the House lights fade, the stage lights come up, the tabs open. Noises stop, but because another element of space and air has been added (the stage and the area that surrounds it) those acoustical qualities change. The ear has to make an immediate adjustment in its ability to receive those fresh sounds, and if the opening lines are not well projected they are lost forever.

In the second instance, the audience has also to become attuned to the individual vocal qualities of all the players involved. This takes time, and you would be well advised to emphasise this point to your cast.

Dialects and accents can create difficulties, so one must be certain of the degree to which these need to be used.

Certainly if the locale requires the players to adopt, say, a regional accent, it is far better for them to *suggest* the rhythm, the placing of the vowel, the stress on the consonant, rather than to attempt to 'ape' the dialect completely. It is rare that players are wholly successful and a poor attempt creates confusion. Another factor is that a strong regional dialect, if truthfully followed, may be incomprehensible to *your* audience, so a compromise has to be reached.

There are certain 'cod' accents which should be avoided. For example, the over-melodic 'look-you' travesty of the Welsh, the thick, coarse, over-stressed guttural 'sure and begorrah' that is stage Irish, the clipped, rolling, reverberating 'R' sounds of the caricatured Scot. These are generalisations, fine for the comedian, but rarely suitable for a credible characterisation. There are many variations in dialect, and the records available from the B.B.C. are a great asset when research is required.

When I am directing a play which calls for a variation of dialect, I make a point of insisting that *all conversation at rehearsal*, both on and off stage, is given that adjustment, and this includes any comments that I contribute. Not an easy task, but I do find that everyone adapts easily and mistakes are more easily spotted.

Where the play is set in a foreign country, say France, and *all* the characters are of that race, I see no point in imposing a phony 'broken' accent on the cast. If truth is to be followed, in reality the cast should speak pure French, but considering if they did so, few of the audience would understand them, it is far better for the French nature of the characters to be shown by their customs, movements and gestures. Obviously, if the main characters are English, and the play is set in England, but with a Frenchman in the plot, it is essential to stress the contrast.

The tone of voice which is used is extremely indicative of our feelings and attitudes, for example, the flat sound of disinterest, the spark which shows excitement, the sharp edge of sarcasm, the warmth of love, the cold note that can strike fear, and so on. A player must be aware of the effect of such vocal variation, and it is here that your guidance is such a help to them.

Some players, for example, have a tendency to be unaware of the required variation of inflection, particularly at the ends of sentences. It is an irritating habit and will destroy the worth of the dialogue. What happens is that at the end of each sentence the inflection is dropped. In effect, every line of the text becomes a statement, whereas in reality there should be the query, the hope, the triumph, and all manners of expressing our emotions.

Let us consider a speech from *Mary Stuart* by Schiller, Act 3, Scene 5.

Mary is considering a meeting which she has just had with Queen Elizabeth, her mortal enemy. The meeting was a fiery one, and was witnessed by Leicester, one of Elizabeth's favourites, but who has been, at one time, Mary's lover.

MARY: Yes! I humbled her before the eyes of Leicester!
           He saw it, he was witness of my triumph.
           And when I put her down from the high place
           He stood near by, his presence gave me strength.

Consider that speech, with every line finishing on a downward, diminishing inflection. It conveys nothing but a bitter woman who feels no joy in her success. Yet, though she may regret it later, *at this moment* she is excited by her meeting with Elizabeth and triumphant about the manner in which she hurled insults and defiance at her adversary. So the euphoria will 'lift' the inflection, will demonstrate exactly what she feels and if the final word, 'strength', is *pointed* it conveys the mad surge of power that she feels.

Lack of RATE and PACE are two criticisms that are often levelled by an adjudicator. The production drags and fails to achieve the 'shape' for which you are aiming.

As a *general* rule, though there are always exceptions, a Director must remember that when the emotions are deepseated and held beneath the surface it is very difficult to express them. Consider a friend having to break the news of the death of a wife to the husband; he feels the burden of responsibility and dreads the task; he is hesitant, choosing his words with care, the natural flow of speech is halted. But once the restraint is broken, and the pent-up feelings are released, the rate and pace increase until a climax is reached.

Consider the following scene from the play *Enter a Free Man* by Tom Stoppard.

George Riley, an inventor of useless artefacts, is trying to tell his wife, Persephone, that he is going to leave her for another woman. Persephone doesn't understand: she is a simple woman, he is a simple man, such things are not part of their conception of life. They both want to say so much, but the uncomfortable restraint is there, there are pauses and hesitations – I have marked them with strokes – which convey the pressures.

ACT TWO. (Extract)

RILEY: Look, there's something else. / I didn't want to say anything in front of Linda.

PERSEPHONE: What do you mean? /

RILEY: I don't want to keep anything from you. / I want to be fair.

PERSE: You're always fair, George.

RILEY: Well . . . / there's this other woman.

PERSE: I beg your pardon, George?

RILEY: / Another woman.

PERSE: Which other woman?

RILEY: What? . . . / You don't know her.

PERSE: Who?

RILEY: The other woman, dammit . . . / you know.

PERSE: / I see. /

RILEY: Yes. /

PERSE: / Since when?

RILEY: Since yesterday.

PERSE: / Since yesterday.

RILEY: / I met her in the pub.

PERSE: Did you?
RILEY: / She knows what I'm trying to do, you see. / We have this understanding.
PERSE: / What understanding?
RILEY: / Spiritual you could call it.
PERSE: Spiritual.
RILEY: / I just thought you ought to know. (PAUSE) Well / I'll be writing, I expect.
PERSE: / Don't get too warm carrying all that stuff. It's really hot again today. / Perhaps you could leave your coat at home.
RILEY: I'll be needing it later. / The weather will change.
PERSE: Of course, there is that . . . / Goodbye, then . . .

So he departs, with nothing really said; perhaps the most significant line is where Persephone shows her love and her force of habit when she makes the remark about his coat. The emotion is still tied within her, but a few minutes later her daughter, Linda, comes in and tells her mother that *she* is leaving home to go off with a boyfriend. After a few comments, Persephone explodes in anger and distress, all those pent-up emotions come pouring out, her reaction to years of frustration in trying to keep the home together.

If that first section is taken without the inner hesitancy, the contrast in the second section will not be given due emphasis. Another point to remember, though it doesn't apply to these extracts, is that when directing a really strong argument you must consider exactly how important each line is. Very often it is the *heat* and pace of the argument that is important, the fact that there is a shouting match going on. Too often the protagonists in stage arguments wait for each line to be fully delivered before they pick up the cues, and the pace is too weak for the fire to be suggested. If you have to deal with such an example, make sure the 'topping' technique is used by the players; (each player making sure that they put over their argument without waiting for the other to finish). You will discover which part of the text is the section that the audience must hear, while the unimportant lines can be almost lost in the cut and thrust of realism.

There are instances where intense feelings are masked by a façade and it is up to the Director to see that the falsity is exposed by taking care to time the delivery of the text. An excellent example is this scene from *A Man For All Seasons* by Robert Bolt, Act 2, Scene 7.

The scene is set in the Tower of London, where Sir Thomas More has been a prisoner for some time. He and his family know that he will be executed if he doesn't concur with Henry VIII's Reformation of the Church. The family come to see him for the last time. His wife, Alice, is not a woman who expresses herself easily and More knows this. At this moment he, too, finds it hard to say what is in his heart. It is easier for him to talk to his daughter, Margaret.

> MORE: Now listen, you must all leave the country.
> MARGARET: And leave you here?
> MORE: It makes no difference, Meg; they won't let you see me again. You must all go on the same day, but not on the same boat: different boats from different ports.
> MARGARET: After the trial, then.
> MORE: There's to be no trial, they have no case. / Do this, I beseech you?
> MARGARET: / Yes.
> MORE: Alice? (SHE TURNS HER BACK) / Alice. I command it.

ALICE: (HARSHLY) Right. (A PAUSE)
MORE: (LOOKING IN THE BASKET OF FOOD THEY HAVE BROUGHT HIM.) Oh. / This is splendid; I know who packed this.
ALICE: (HARSHLY) I packed it.
MORE: / Yes . . . / You still make superlative custard, Alice.
ALICE: Do I?
MORE: / That's a nice dress you have on.
ALICE: It's my cooking dress.
MORE: It's very nice, anyway. / Nice colour.
ALICE: (TURNING TO HIM) By God, you think very little of me. (WITH MOUNTING BITTERNESS) / I know I'm a fool. But I'm not such a fool as at this time to be lamenting for my dresses . . . or to relish compliments on my custard. (PAUSE)
MORE: I am well rebuked.

The scene continues but now More is able to express his fears, and Alice her bitterness because she cannot understand why he must die for his beliefs. He pleads with her for her understanding, and she holds him and replies . . .

ALICE: Sh . . . As for understanding, I understand that you're the best man I've ever met or am ever likely to, and if you go . . . well Heaven knows why, I suppose . . . though Heaven's my witness, Heaven's kept deadly quiet about it. And if anyone wants my opinion of the King and his Council, they have only to ask for it.
MORE: Why, it's a lion I married, a lion . . . A lion! A lion! (PAUSE) . . . Say what you may, this custard's good. It's very good.

93

Study of this scene will reveal how the performances are required on two levels . . . the one that is spoken, and the one that is not, and it is the unspoken one that really predominates.

TIMING of dialogue requires a great deal of technical study, and is certainly not learnt from books. Some players, however, have a natural ear and an ability to phrase a line and 'point' a word. A Director cannot easily impose the precision required, but if you are able to guide a player to the interpretation that you feel is correct, you will find that an enthusiastic and intelligent player will respond.

Here are a few examples where the pause, and the 'pointing' help to clarify the meaning of the text. In *A Phoenix Too Frequent* by Christopher Fry, a widow is describing her late husband . . . and his abilities . . . !

'He made balance sheets sound like Homer, / and Homer / sound like balance sheets!'

The contrast and humour will be stressed if the first line is intoned with praise and the second with dismay, and almost 'thrown away'.

In Oscar Wilde's *The Importance of Being Earnest*, two young society girls, both under the illusion that they are engaged to the same man, sit and share afternoon tea. The code of society prevents them being outwardly rude, but the whole scene demonstrates their rivalry. Again, I have indicated the pauses, the slight hesitations, with strokes.

CECILY: Do you suggest, Miss Fairfax, that I entrapped Ernest into an engagement? / How dare you? This is no time for wearing the shallow mask of manners. / When I see a spade, I call it a spade.

GWENDOLINE: I am glad to say / that I have never seen / a spade. / It is obvious / that our social spheres have been widely/different.

By phrasing the dialogue with care, the maximum bite is assured, which is the purpose of the text at that point. And so it continues. At a later point –

CECILY: . . . May I offer you tea, Miss Fairfax?
GWENDOLINE: Thank you. (WITH ELABOR-ATE POLITENESS) (ASIDE) Detestable girl! But I require tea!
CECILY: (SWEETLY) Sugar?
GWENDOLINE: (SUPERCILIOUSLY) No thank you. 'Sugar' is not fashionable any more.

(CECILY LOOKS ANGRILY AT HER, TAKES UP THE TONGS AND PUTS FOUR LUMPS IN THE CUP.)

CECILY: Cake or bread and butter?
GWENDOLINE: (BORED MANNER) Bread and butter, please. 'Cake' is rarely seen at the *best* houses nowadays.

(CECILY CUTS A VERY LARGE SLICE OF CAKE AND PUTS IT ON THE TRAY. TO THE BUTLER SHE ORDERS . . .)

CECILY: Hand that to Miss Fairfax . . .

Of course, in this instance, it is essential to consider the STYLE of delivery. Just as we considered the STYLE of Movement, equally a Director must define the STYLE of speech, and when dealing with period plays – whether they are Shakespearean tragedies, Restoration comedies or historical plays written by modern authors – they each call for a definition of style. It is essential that you are able to differentiate between a text that requires sincerity and one that calls for artificiality. For example, an Elizabethan tragedy will require sincerity, but artificiality would be called for in a Restoration Comedy of Manners.

It is the ability to phrase the sentences of the dialogue that will really make or mar the performance of the player. Too often, insufficient care is taken in conveying the true meaning of the text. This is particularly noticeable when the player has to deal with large speeches. There is a tendency to whip through them quickly, without ascertaining the best approach, the best delivery.

Long speeches need to be broken up into relevant passages; marking the sections that need to be stressed, emphasised, and the degree of emphasis required. How best to 'point' certain lines, certain words – which passage is the important one, which can be technically 'thrown away' – these should be made clear. The clues are there and should be sought.

Thus, in this fashion and with the co-operation of the players, you will discover through study and rehearsal the most suitable and profitable way in which to guide and direct the human voice into a true illumination of the dialogue. The characters will become more than mere skeletons of 'John Brown', their relationships will begin to intrigue, and gradually you should be achieving the 'shape' of the play, and building towards that completed jigsaw.

Chapter Eleven

'THE CLUES ARE THERE . . . SEEK THEM.'

It is not easy to sustain the credibility of the character throughout rehearsals and performance. You will find that, even with the best intentions in the world, there is a tendency for 'John Brown' to slip back into his own manner of speech and movement.

This danger must be avoided, and it is up to the director to ensure that the many facets of character are maintained. It is at this stage of rehearsals that the dialogue is constantly revealing new factors that may well affect the interpretation of the script, certainly the performances. It is advisable to watch and listen most carefully. This is where that production secretary really proves the worth of the position! Too many directors tend to sit with their noses in the script, eyes only for the odd paraphrasing or missed cue. A prompt is there to watch for such details, a production secretary should keep an eye on the text and on your notes, and be prepared to catch any comments that you wish to be reminded of when that particular section of the rehearsal is over. By now, you should not be interrupting the cast more than is absolutely necessary; far better to keep the continuity going with one part of that 'jigsaw', then re-rehearse it in the light of your response to what you have seen and heard.

The character relationships should, by now, be clearly

defined and expressed within the situation that is developing. By relationships, I am obviously not referring to the position of the characters in terms of kinship, e.g. brother, sister, aunt, etc., but in the manner of their connection within the given circumstances of the situation. Again let us look at that 'imaginary play' and use it as an example:

(a) Martha and Mary are of the same status in the house, both being maids, but Mary has a secret hold over Martha, remember, and this will give her a certain amount of power, which can be expressed in the manner of speech she adopts when speaking to Martha.

(b) John is in love with Jane, nevertheless Jane is more wary in her communications with him, since she does not want him to discover the truth about her past. During their love scenes, however, she may be so emotionally moved that she nearly forgets her fears, thus John may gently probe her responses, for he is slightly perplexed.

(c) Ralph is the master, Mary the servant; but, because she is blackmailing him, there will be an underlying lack of respect on her part, in her acceptance of his orders. This must be expressed in a subtle manner. Undue emphasis would create early suspicions in the mind of the audience, and would, therefore, spoil the ultimate dénouement.

If your study of the script is thorough, these relationships will be clear, even through change of situation and of circumstances; remember there are always times when we alter our opinion of someone!

Some writers appear to give very few clues about atti-

98

tudes, but further research and imagination on the part of the director and the cast will answer most queries.

Let us look at the works of William Shakespeare, and *The Merchant of Venice* in particular.

The main character is Antonio, the eponymous merchant. We understand that he is of sound business acumen, though at the moment his ships, which represent all his capital, are embarking on rough seas. His friend Bassanio requires a loan in order to court the fair lady Portia, and, since Antonio has always helped his friends in the past, he is prepared to seek a loan from the money-lending Jew, Shylock.

When the play opens, Antonio is with two of his friends, Salerio and Solanio . . .

ANTONIO: In sooth, I know not why I am so sad.
It wearies me; you say it wearies you;
But how I caught it, found it, or came by it,
What stuff 'tis made of, whereof it is born,
I am to learn.
And such a want-wit sadness makes of me
That I have much ado to know myself.

Obviously, from the content of the first line, we know that he is replying to a question, the important 'gone-before'. The answer must be direct. He is weary of his mood, irritated by it. He is also vexed by the question and the questioner.

A few moments later, he denies that he is concerned for his merchandise, and scorns the idea that he is in love. He does not know the reason for his depression. In colloquial terms, he is 'fed up' without knowing why.

In that opening speech, if the actor is too concerned with the sadness, the low mood is too prolonged and gives a dull start to the act. Antonio is rather a solemn character throughout the whole play, but you should seek the opportunity to show another facet of the man.

Before continuing, let us stop for a moment and have another look at the term 'the gone-before'. As I said in a previous chapter, the characters and the situation exist within a time span, but what has occurred earlier is of major importance and is a dominant factor in determining the attitudes of everyone concerned.

Yet another example from *The Merchant of Venice*. Another major character is Portia. She is heiress to a fortune, but is bound by her father's will to marry only a suitor who solves the riddle of three caskets, each containing either gold, silver or lead. She is made of stronger mettle than she may appear to be on the surface, and later in the play adopts the guise of an advocate in an effort to save Antonio's life. Her most famous speech is, of course, 'The Quality of Mercy' speech in Act 4, Scene 1:

> The quality of mercy is not strained;
> It droppeth as the gentle rain from Heaven
> Upon the place beneath. It is twice blest;
> It blesseth him that gives and him that takes,
> 'Tis mightiest in the mightiest; it becomes
> The throned monarch better than his crown;
> His sceptre shows the force of temporal power,
> The attribute to awe and majesty,
> Wherein doth sit the dread and fear of kings,
> It is an attribute to God Himself;
> And earthly power doth then show likest God's
> When mercy seasons justice . . .

Many directors forget that she is in the court as an *advocate* and they allow this speech to be delivered in sweet entreaties. But such an approach would not deceive anyone and would certainly not stir Shylock into his sharp retort –

> My deeds upon my head! I crave the law!

She has not persuaded him to relent, but she has stirred the court by making him openly declare his anger and his hatred of the Christians.

Now let us look at two more characters from the same play, this time the two young lovers, Jessica and Lorenzo. In Act 5, Scene 1, they wait for Portia's return and sit in the garden watching the moonlight.

LORENZO: The moon shines bright. In such a night as this,
When the sweet wind did gently kiss the trees,
And they did make no noise . . . in such a night,
Troilus methinks mounted the Troyan walls,
And sigh'd his soul towards the Grecian tents,
Where Cressid lay that night.

JESSICA: In such a night
Did Thisby fearfully oe'rtrip the dew,
And saw the lion's shadow ere himself,
And ran dismayed away.

LORENZO: In such a night
Stood Dido with a willow in her hand
Upon the wild sea banks, and waft her love,
To come again to Carthage.

JESSICA: In such a night
              Medea gathered the enchanted herbs
              That did renew old Aeson.

LORENZO: In such a night
              Did Jessica steal from the wealthy Jew,
              And with an unthrift love did run from
                  Venice
              As far as Belmont.

JESSICA: In such a night
              Did young Lorenzo swear he lov'd her well,
              Stealing her soul with many vows of faith,
              And ne'er a true one.

LORENZO: In such a night
              Did pretty Jessica, like a little shrew,
              Slander her love, and he forgave it her.

JESSICA: I would out-night you, did nobody come:
              But hark, I hear the footing of a man.

This is a delightful text, starting off on a serious note, but gradually changing into a teasing mood as the two lovers try to out-wit each other. If sentimentality is over-stressed, it becomes sickly and boring, but here are two young people, freshly stirred in the manner of physical love, and the clue to the mood is in the line:

        I would out-night *you*, did nobody come.

On this occasion a light, physical contact would illuminate the innocent sexuality of the moment.

Many groups are wary of tackling the works of Shakespeare. They think reverently of 'The Bard' and worry about the difficulties of pentametrical verse.

    I find it a great help to remind them that Will Shakespeare

was a country youth, who married a woman older than himself, and deserted her and their children to go to London. There he became an actor and proceeded to live a very full life of wine, women and song, dying at the early age of 52 years. During this period he produced such literary masterpieces that they have been acclaimed the world over, *but* he was a man with human frailties and failings, and he was conveying so much of his experiences of life through his writing.

His characters are not pale shadows, but full-blooded humans. If his plays are interpreted not as rare relics that we fear to tackle, but as the practical theatrical gifts from which we gain, and give pleasure, then we bestow our appreciation in a spirit of which Shakespeare would have approved.

The question of any play in verse does worry the inexperienced director, but once you are sure of the meaning of the lines and the quality of the writing it is no more difficult than handling any other script.

Take, for example, the opening of a modern verse play, *A Phoenix Too Frequent* by Christopher Fry.

The main character, Dynamene, is mourning her husband in his tomb, as was the custom. She is determined to stay there till death claims her. She has a companion with her, their maid, Doto, a simple country girl who, while she is aware of her loyalties and duties, is not in the least keen to perish in this fashion, or at this time of her life. As the play opens, the widow is asleep, and Doto muses on her fortunes and her fears. The text reveals both:

DOTO:	Nothing but the harmless day gone into black	1
	Is all the night is. And so what's my trouble?	2

Demons is so much wind . . . are so much
   wind. 3
I've plenty to fill my thoughts. All that I ask 4
Is don't keep turning men over in my mind, 5
Venerable Aphrodite. I've had my last one 6
And thank you, I thank thee. He smelt of
   sour grass 7
And was likeable. He collected ebony
   quoits. 8

(AN OWL HOOTS NEAR AT HAND)

O Zeus! O some god or other, where is the
   oil? 9
Fire's from Prometheus. I thank thee. If I 10
Mean to do die I'd better see what I'm doing. 11

(SHE FILLS THE LAMP WITH OIL)

Honestly, I would rather have to sleep 12
With a bald bee keeper who was wearing his
   boots 13
Than spend more days fasting and thirsting
   and crying 14
In a tomb. I shouldn't have said that. Pretend 15
I didn't hear myself. But life and death 16
Is cat and dog in this double bed of a world. 17
My master, my poor master, was a man 18
Whose nose was as straight as a little buttress 19
And now he's taken it into Elysium 20
Where it won't be noticed among all the other
   straightness. 21

(THE OWL HOOTS AGAIN)

> Oh. Them owls . . . those owls. It's woken
> her.   22

Here is a perfect example of the required 'breaking up' of a speech into the relevant phrases, which express so much of her fears and her attempts to overcome them. This is well demonstrated in lines, 1, 2, 3, and 9, 10 and 11.

Her grammatical lapses, which she realises and tries to remedy are evident in lines 3, 7 and 22, her sexual torment in lines 4 and 5, her reminiscences of sex in 7 and 8, her simple philosophical thoughts in 15, 16 and 17, and her thoughts on her late master in lines 18, 19, 20 and 21.

A very amusing character: clear-cut, and one who sets the light tone of a play which is in sharp contrast to its subject matter.

In this last example, the character makes many changes of mood, but it is a light flow from one to the other as her mind tries to settle to the situation in which she finds herself. There are occasions when the change has to be more direct, more forceful.

Note the following speech from *Mary Stuart*, Act 2, Scene 1. Lord Burleigh is asking Elizabeth I to agree to the death of Mary Stuart. There is much contrast in the approach to the delivery of each line:

ELIZABETH: What is it that my people still
    demand?
BURLEIGH: The head of Mary Stuart. If you
    would give   1
    The precious gift of freedom to your
    people   2
    And make secure for them their hard
    won faith,   3

The head of Mary Stuart must fall. If we	4
Are not to live to live endlessly apprehensive	5
Whilst in the dark of Fotheringay Castle	6
That witch still conjures plots and tries	7
To set this land ablaze with her love torch	8
Her head must fall.	9
For her, young men go gladly to sure death.	10
They dream of freeing her. But what she claims	11
Is nothing else except your throne.	12
There can be no peace with a Stuart.	13
She lives, you die. She dies . . . and you will live.	14

The first four lines are quietly persuasive, but during lines 5 to 9 there is a gradual building of power and tension, even though 6, 7 and 8 have almost to be 'thrown away'; then the final lines must stress the contrasts as he condemns Mary and her claims, and warns Elizabeth of the consequences of delay. The clue here really lies in the last line. It is a simple fact that Burleigh must stress.

A play which deals with Elizabeth I when she was much younger is *The Young Elizabeth* by Jennette Dowling and Francis Letton.

At the end of the first act, Elizabeth is in virtual imprisonment at Hatfield House. The Young Edward is on the throne, but the country is really under the firm rule of Somerset, who has named himself Lord Protector. Somerset sends two of his supporters to Hatfield to try to get Elizabeth to confess that she has been engaged in adulterous activities with Sir Thomas Seymour, and has also been conspiring with him to take the throne from Edward. The two investigators are Lord and Lady Tyrwhitt, and they are merciless in their enquiries. At one stage they arrange for Elizabeth's old servants to be taken to the Tower and tortured in order that they may give false evidence against her. The scene is one of verbal battle throughout, and should be taken as such. The clue here is in a line of Tyrwhitt's when he expresses his frustration in anger . . .

> TYRWHITT: Your Grace, I am done with *duelling with words*.

That reveals exactly how the rate and pace, the whole tone of the scene must be played. There are cut and thrusts – though there *are* respites, just brief ones, when strength is gathered again after one thrust has failed, or when one thrust has cut deeply.

The act ends with a most dramatically effective scene, which must be handled with great care if the whole of the preceding scene is not to be spoilt.

After much of the duel, a message comes from London that Thomas Seymour has been beheaded. The Tyrwhitts are triumphant – surely Elizabeth will now speak – they have her where they want her!

> TYRWHITT: 'And do you communicate to the Lady Elizabeth's Grace, that this day of March the 20th, in the year of our Lord fifteen forty-nine, for reasons of high treason against the King, Lord Thomas Seymour died upon the scaffold, his head being severed from his body.'

(ELIZABETH DOES NOT MOVE. HER EYES SEEM TO GO FROM TYRWHITT TO BEYOND THE WALLS. THERE IS SILENCE.)

Can you say nothing to that?
LADY TYRWHITT: (AFTER A PAUSE.) Nothing?

(THERE IS A LONG SILENCE. THEN ELIZABETH LOOKS SLOWLY TO TYRWHITT. WHEN SHE SPEAKS SHE UTTERS EACH WORD CLEARLY FOR ITSELF ALONE.)

ELIZABETH: This day died a man of great wit, and little wisdom.

(TYRWHITT'S MOUTH ALMOST DROPS OPEN. HIS WIFE HOLDS UP HER HANDS IN DEFEAT. THEY BOTH EXIT.)
(THERE IS A SHORT SILENCE. THEN ELIZABETH RISES. WHEN SHE SPEAKS, IN THE TORRENT OF HER GRIEF IS ALL HER LOVE FOR THOMAS.)

This day died a man of great wit, and little wisdom. Tom . . . Tom . . .

It is essential that the sorrow that Elizabeth feels is understood by the actress: any superficial performance or rushing of the dialogue will destroy the whole atmosphere. The first part of her line will show the courage of a future Queen. The sorrow-laden distress of the repeat shows the heartbreak of a woman.

And this is a scene ending when the lights should *slowly*

fade and the main tabs *slowly* close, and then a brief pause before the House lights are *slowly* brought up to full.

I must confess that I am always excited by the discoveries that close study and rehearsal of the text bring, and if you can inspire the cast with your excitement you are on the right road to seeing the play really take shape.

There are going to be occasions when your endeavours appear to fail. You must be prepared for that, but if everyone is really contributing wholeheartedly, it may be just a breather before that final push.

For your part, it's the opportunity for close reconsideration of your contribution to the production; perhaps certain scenes need a little embellishment?

Chapter Twelve

ORIGINALITY AND EMBELLISHMENT

To use the simile of a jigsaw puzzle is good enough for the basics of production and direction, but one needs to look a little further than that one-dimensional picture. It is certainly a process by which you can create your own understanding of a written text, to reproduce that picture on the box. However, early in rehearsal and during your studies you may instinctively feel that there are certain sections that are weaker than others. It may be in the writing; such things happen. It may be in the performance given by the player, but it may be that there is a vital spark missing that you, the Director, should supply!

It is not easy to assess your own contribution, but you should look for the individual touch of creativity which puts your personal mark on the whole production, though of course I do not advocate futile gimmickry merely to demonstrate your originality. A great deal will depend on the text and on what you have achieved during rehearsal.

Obviously, if your approach to the piece has been audacious and contrasts with the normally accepted conventional interpretation of the script, you would have set this approach from the beginning, and it would certainly be too late to introduce such ideas at this stage. I am referring to the average straightforward production which seems to require some theatrical 'lift'.

It is important to remember that you must respect the laws of copyright. To alter or delete any texts without the permission of the writer or the writer's agent is illegal. This law also covers the illegality of photo-copying the text. This is, regrettably, a crime which occurs only too frequently nowadays, particularly in the amateur theatre. It is a crime since it robs the writer of part of his/her income. If you wish to make alterations or deletions, simply apply to the copyright agent whose name is always included in the frontispiece of the script.

However excellent a script is, there are always moments when your creative imagination is needed to supply a few moments of magic. However excellent a script is, there are many instances when the writer is not familiar with theatrical practice as regards staging that work. It is not always politic for a writer to give precise instructions about the staging and production. They are concerned with the *written* text, it is up to you to bring it to life in your own individual manner.

Take for instance, a play like Alan Bennett's *Habeas Corpus*. It is described as a satirical merry-go-round, and there we meet a family and their friends for whom the determination to put sex and the satisfaction of the body first is the ruling passion of their lives. It is a text which requires much flair on the part of the director. Set on a bare stage, furnished only with three chairs, the characters weave in and out of a series of mistaken identities and sexual encounters.

Mrs Swabb, an aptly-named family charwoman, would appear to be the 'chorus', since, as she goes about her cleaning tasks, she comments upon and introduces the various characters and the situations in which they become entangled. They are:

Dr Arthur Wickstead	a medical man, always lusting, but rarely after . . .
Muriel Wickstead	his wife, although she is always open to offers.
Dennis Wickstead	their son, whose future is weak and whose experience is none.
Constance Wickstead	his aunt, who is flat chested and seeks an expansion . . . a falsie. She is engaged to . . .
Canon Throbbing	He is frustrated, but ever hopeful.
Felicity	engaged to Dennis, but not averse to offers from his father.

The cast numbers eleven in all, but this list gives an idea of the style of play and the characters that are involved.

If the text, most of which is written in blank verse or doggerel, is delivered without thought of theatrical invention of movement and stage business, there is a danger that the play will lose its intended impact. The whole pattern of movement needs choreographing as in dance, and the three chairs can be put to a variety of uses.

Sound effects, including a wide range of carefully chosen music, add to the dimensions of the production.

When I directed this play some years ago, I used 'Hard Day's Night' by the Beatles as introductory music, 'The Stripper' by David Rose to accompany Muriel's attempted seduction of the 'falsie' fitter who had come to give Constance her required 'expansion', and the tango 'Jealousy' to accompany Constance's dance with another character. At the end of the play, there is a marriage ceremony between

Dennis and Felicity. Mrs Swabb comments throughout, and is later followed by Arthur Wickstead making a speech which sums up his thoughts on sex.

According to the writer, the rest of the cast gradually exit during this speech and leave Arthur alone on stage. Here, I felt, was another moment which would need a theatrical flourish, though none was suggested in the script. However, I used a recording of 'The Wedding March' by Mendelssohn and arranged with the effects technician to introduce it at the correct speed just prior to the 'ceremony'. The wedding party paired and processed round the happy couple in the manner of a formal dance. Gradually the speed of the record was increased, and with the added effect of a 'strobe' light, which gives a flickering effect, the couples appeared to be whirled off stage one by one, as the pace quickened and the pitch of music rose high.

When they were all off stage except Mrs Swabb and Arthur Wickstead, the music faded, the lights dimmed to two spots, and they again faded when the characters had concluded their final speeches.

For the curtain call, which followed, I had the same record but with the speed reversed. It started high pitched and fast, the couples were whirled on stage and as it slowed down the cast all fell into line for the benefit of the audience. It meant extra work in rehearsal and great precision in the timing of music and movement, but well worth the effort, and as the cast all skipped off à la Morecambe and Wise, the audience responded with glee!

On another occasion, I was directing *Sweeney Todd* by Brian J. Burton. This was to be the theatre's Christmas production as a change from the usual pantomime, but I still wanted to retain the atmosphere of a show that would delight and entertain the whole family. I wanted to use colour, song and dance to match the festive season.

The story of the 'Demon Barber of Fleet Street' is too well known for me to relate here. The text covers both dialogue and lyrics, for there are a few simple songs to be sung by the cast, mostly solos. Here again I felt that more elaboration was required, and sought ways in which this could be done without in any manner interfering with the writer's intention. Brian J. Burton, when approached, generously gave me permission for a few cuts in dialogue to enable me to spend extra time on the inclusion of several production numbers.

The opening scene takes place outside Sweeney Todd's shop in Fleet Street, London, so I felt it was quite legitimate to include extras here: characters walking about enjoying the evening air, buying or selling wares, such as hot chestnuts, crumpets, flowers, etc., or, maybe, just gossiping. I included in the crowd young Tobias Ragg and his mother having a heated conversation (sotto voce), for shortly afterwards Tobias is taken to Sweeney Todd as an apprentice, and I thought it was a good idea to introduce him and the fact that he was reluctant to take the job.

I also included six sailors, mingling with the crowd. These are not included in the cast list, but since Mark Ingestre, the hero, is a naval officer just home from foreign shores, and since the first song Tobias sings is called 'Sailing Away', I felt that there was sufficient licence for their presence!

All the extras on stage were able to add vocal backing to Todd's first song, 'I'm Sweeney Todd the Barber', with the slight alteration of the lyric, and joined with Tobias in his song. Both numbers were choreographed to create simple dances in which the sailors and the extras joined. Thus, the production opened on a note of bustle and activity which made for a strong contrast to the following scene when Sweeney Todd and Tobias are alone, and the mood is rather sinister.

Since this is a script which comes under the convention of theatricality rather than realism, it is ideal material for embellishment.

Later in the play, Tobias is in trouble; he is being held a prisoner in a madhouse. He sings a song appealing to Heaven for help – all is dark – he is frightened, but, of course, help does come. I exploited the situation by having 'angels' (the dancers) come to comfort him in his sorrow. A few appeared from the wings, out of the darkness, but the remainder flew in on wires. Those on the ground danced, while the others were joined by a heavenly chorus singing off stage in answer to the poor boy's plea. The whole episode was received with delight, and was much applauded.

There is also a scene where the inmates of Newgate Prison sing a little ditty called 'Down in the Jug'. It is very short, two four-line verses. I felt this was a piece that could be profitably expanded. I wrote six more verses – all relevant to characters who were in prison for various offences: stealing, soliciting for prostitution, non-payment of debts, assault and battery, wife-beating, murder, etc. The six characters, poorly dressed in filthy rags, and wearing prison shackles, shuffled on, sang their appropriate verse, joined with the others in the chorus, and did a little dance. The dance was difficult since they had to drag around their chains, but it proved to be hilarious and received many requests for an encore. However, I believe in leaving an audience asking for more!

On another occasion, and in an entirely contrasting mood, I was rather perplexed over the staging of the execution scene (Act 5, Scene 6) from *Mary Stuart*. The actual execution is taking place in an adjoining room, but the Earl of Leicester has been ordered to witness Mary's death. He stands alone watching from the door, and describes the

115

scene. Since he has been Mary's lover in the past, he is reluctant to be present, but has to conform to the will of Elizabeth I, who has made the order. He speaks thus . . .

LEICESTER: She moves toward her death, spirit
transcendent,
And I stay tangled here among the
damned.
What life from Heaven I have cast away!
What has become of my determination
To feel nothing, see nothing, but my
aims,
Look on with unmoved eyes when her
head falls?
Did her glance waken me to shame?
And must her death ensnare me now
with love?
No, that's too late. She's gone. You are
earthbound
You must pursue your gross aims to the
end.
Make your heart heartless, watch with
stony eyes
Her death, so you may gain your
shameful prize.
I have to see her die. I was sent here as
witness.

(HE MOVES TOWARD THE DOOR OF THE EXECUTION CHAMBER)

In vain! My eyes are dazed! I cannot
watch
Her death! I hear voices.

116

> I hear the Dean admonish her. She
>   interrupts.
> Listen. She prays. It seems so loud.
> So strong,
> Her voice. Now all is quiet. Quite still.
> I hear
> Only a sobbing from her women. Now
>   they bare her neck.
> The block is brought. She kneels down.
> Lays her head.

(HE COLLAPSES FAINTING. AT THE SAME
TIME A LOUD CRY IS HEARD FROM BELOW.)

However well the actor conveyed the feelings of the character, it was as if he were acting in a vacuum. After a little
thought, I decided to stage the execution in the wings, with
the characters involved, as they would have been if we were
actually present. There were noises off; Mary praying in
Latin; the Dean admonishing her; the crying of women; the
noise of the block being brought; the axe falling and the
final scream. This was well controlled for volume, and was
never allowed to override Leicester's speech. The only light
on stage was reflected from the wings and falling on the
actor's face; this created shadows on the walls, and the
effect gradually changed to red at the final scream before
fading to black.

The whole scene gained from the added dimension and
it gave the actor a deeper understanding of his rôle. Need-
less to say, the only thing that was chopped off stage was a
large cabbage: I really couldn't afford to replace Mary Stuart
for every performance!

You may be faced with a problem of staging, and need

117

ingenuity and enterprise to find a solution. Very often a play which requires a complexity of presentation is discarded for this very reason, which is a pity.

It should be realised that it is not essential to reproduce every detail of a locale, even in a realistic convention. The audience will accept a suggestion of a set, and their imagination will build the complete picture. It is, after all, *the play* that is being presented. Scenery is merely a background and with careful use of lighting equipment, the action can switch from one locale to another, and a screen, or a piece of furniture will suffice.

Over the years, I have seen many imaginative settings where simplicity has been the very effective keynote. This was particularly noticeable in One-Act Drama Festivals, where the elements of time and transport make intricate scenery inadvisable. In these Festivals, the performance has to take place mainly in a Curtain Set of stage drapes, although certain additions are allowed. What is important, however, is that the entire stage must be 'set' in no more than 10 minutes, and 'struck' in no more than 5 minutes. If excess time is taken, marks are deducted. Even in a Full Length Play Festival, it must be remembered that the complete setting has to be erected, lit, furnished in one day, and then immediately 'struck' after the performance and transported from the theatre.

It's surprising how imagination springs; I can remember all of these simple and effective sets:

1. A production of Edward Albee's play *The American Dream*, where the entire house was a mere skeletal framework with the window frames and doors suspended from the overhead bars.
2. A ship's deck for the play *Was He Anyone* by N. F.

Simpson suggested by the use of white ropes, a lifebelt and rostra.

3. A churchyard scene from *Mixed Doubles* by David Campton represented by a bench and a plinth topped by a white angel, the latter carefully constructed by 'Props' from wood, wire and papier mâché.

4. Finally, a production of *School for Spinsters* by Molière, where the setting consisted merely of muslin screens painted to represent the frontage of a house. The screens were slid on to a framework, roughly 6' × 4', each screen self-supporting. After the performance this was easily dismantled, the fabric carefully rolled up, and the whole set was ready-packed to take on a plane, since the next performance was to take place in Florida!

Now all these ideas are very simple and quite commonly accepted. What does disappoint many an adjudicator, myself included, are the occasions when it is obvious that little thought or imagination has gone into a presentation. Too many groups fail to use the facilities that are available in the theatre: the lighting equipment, the sky cloth or cyclorama, and the sound equipment. They forget the advantages that the use of rostra can give, the use of traverse curtains, etc.

However, even with a well designed set, sometimes there are changes to be made. Certainly they should be well organised and rehearsed with the stage staff all clad in dark clothes and soft-soled shoes, but there are the odd occasions when you have to make the changes in full view of the audience: for instance, if the production is to be given in a theatre where there is no proscenium arch, and without main tabs. It may be that the text is such that to close those tabs continually would emphasise its fragmentary nature.

HOW TO PRODUCE A PLAY

Look again at *A Man For All Seasons* by Robert Bolt. There are sixteen scenes in the play, and the action moves swiftly, as Sir Thomas More is brought to his death by his determination not to forsake his religious principles.

I decided when I directed the play some time ago, to stage it in a composite setting of rostra at various levels. This was placed U.S. and by lighting the cyclorama in a variety of colours we were able to suggest not only different times of day or night, but to create moods applicable to certain scenes.

The main acting area of the stage was left empty except for four screens. These were constructed to represent heavy Tudor oak timber frames; they each contained 'tapestries' of the period; they were adaptable in the sense that the tapestries could be removed and other detail insets substituted, e.g.

a. Flower-decked trellis for a garden scene.
b. Heavy bars for a prison scene at the Tower of London.
c. Royal banners and Coats of Arms for Westminster Hall.
d. Wattle and daub effect for the inn walls.

The frames were approximately 8′ high and 6′ wide, and the feet were set at right angles to make them self-supporting, and these were 'soled' with carpet so that they slid easily over the stage floor. While the lights 'cross-faded' from one area to another, the frames could be slid off stage by servants and guards dressed in the appropriate Tudor costume, and the insets changed according to the following locale. Furniture was kept to a minimum, a heavy oak table, two Tudor-type chairs, a couple of benches and two large barrels.

The production changes ran very smoothly, having been well organised by the S.M. and her crew.

Different problems were created by the French farce *Hotel Paradiso* by Georges Feydeau. It is a light piece, the humour being created out of mistaken identity in a hotel where various couples had made secret assignations. I felt it required a light, almost chocolate box type of setting and bravura performances to match. The first and third acts take place in the upper room of a house in Paris, period 1910. It has three doors, one from the main entrance of the house, and the other two leading to bedrooms. A practical window is also included – the owner of the house, M. Boniface, uses this when he wishes to escape after his wife has locked him in the room.

The second act is set in the hotel, a slightly seedy building which has seen better days. We needed to represent a reception area with desk, etc., stairs leading from the front of the hotel and continuing to an upper floor, two main bedrooms and a door supposedly leading to another bedroom.

The first main bedroom required furnishing with a double bed, chairs, etc., and also required a fireplace and an exit to a bathroom. The second bedroom required furnishing with five beds (or the impression of five beds) but one has to be practical and capable of being curtained off from the others, and, again, an exit to a bathroom is required.

This second act set must be *visible* from all angles, since in the best tradition of farce there is a considerable amount of action with the cast in and out of the rooms, up and down the stairs. It also has to be of fairly solid construction.

After due consideration, it became obvious that since the theatre had a shallow acting area behind the proscenium arch, but a very deep 'apron' thrust below it, the best way out of the situation was to construct the Hotel set up-stage and play the 1st and 3rd acts on the apron.

We were able to 'inset' the backing for the 1st and 3rd acts within the main acting area and behind the proscenium arch, so that when the tabs were closed the essentials could be struck. The sketch opposite will demonstrate how this was contrived.

Some of the furniture for the 1st and 3rd acts had, by necessity, to be set out front. To remove them in the dark was impossible since they had to be manhandled off stage, down some steps and carried round to the rear of the stage. To tackle the task in full view of the audience in the normal way would have destroyed the mood of the show, and to do it during the interval would have been equally unsatisfactory. The solution came when I decided to make the exercise part of the show: I had the four porters, who later doubled as gendarmes (all part of the cast), come on stage in a little dance in time to the music I used as incidental music for the play. This was Ibert's 'Divertissement' and I used the section entitled 'Valse'. The 'dancers' then proceeded to remove the furniture from the stage as part of a routine. They took it, in time to the music, to the top of the steps, where it was collected by stage staff, also suitably clad. The 'porters' danced off, and once the furniture was out of sight, the house lights came on for the interval. The audience were highly amused at the idea, and doubly delighted when the process was reversed for Act 3 – it gave a real flourish to a successful production.

There are many ways in which you can introduce your own 'flourish' to a production, but *don't* become so involved with the elaboration that you neglect to check that the main principles of the production are sound.

There are many instances where a little imagination, a great deal of thought, and even more effort has created an entirely new concept of presentation and production. The

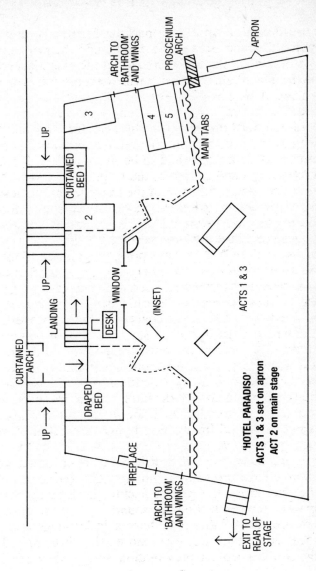

ACT 2. GAUZE FLATS USED WHERE ESSENTIAL TO AVOID MASKING

examples I have used are mere introductions to the fact that in the theatre very little is impossible: as one stage designer once said to me – 'The difficult we do at once, the impossible by lunch-time, but for miracles come back tomorrow!'

Chapter Thirteen

REHEARSAL PRACTICE AND PRINCIPLES

When I am adjudicating I often hear the excuse 'But we only do it for fun!' This is a remark which annoys me intensely, for I believe that if that is the only reason why they indulge themselves in amateur theatricals, they should not subject an audience to their tomfoolery.

Surely it is understood that the higher the standard attained, the greater the enjoyment for all, audience and participants alike. The enjoyment comes equally during the rehearsal process and the performance.

The objective of the early rehearsals is to initiate the ground work of the production as covered in previous chapters. During this stage, the players will be using their scripts not only for reference, but for making essential notes. However, it should be seen that all are making an effort to assimilate the demands of the rôle. It should be made clear that it is not your responsibility as Director to spend time listening as they learn their lines. That task is the 'homework' of the players and should be tackled painstakingly.

Noel Coward used to insist that all his cast were word perfect *prior* to the first rehearsal. This is not a practice I would recommend, for I believe that it imposes a restraint on development, and the deeper understanding of the text.

HOW TO PRODUCE A PLAY

I am frequently asked if I could give advice on the subject of learning dialogue, but there is no hard and fast rule. It all depends on the nature of the text and on the player. Many people underline the words of the character they are portraying and try to absorb them a little at a time. Others find it easier to study the whole page. A tape recording of the lines is an aid to others, who play the tape continually, perhaps when they are pottering around the house and garden or when they are motoring. If this method is a help, it is advisable to prepare a tape in which the cues alone are recorded, leaving sufficient space on the tape for the character lines to be delivered.

The best advice I can give is that the players ensure that they are familiar with *the whole play*; not just every line of dialogue, but its dramatic shape and the purpose of the characters within the situation. By this method, the lines of the character being portrayed seem to fall into place more easily, and greater confidence is gained.

Although there will always be the laggard who is not as familiar with the lines as you would wish, I would still insist that a date is fixed when scripts are put aside. The prompt is there and should be used where necessary; on no account let the other players give the line, this only creates confusion and is bad practice. It can undermine the confidence of the prompt who may begin to feel superfluous.

'Gabble' rehearsals are useful and can be taken by the production secretary while you are, perhaps, engaged in a private rehearsal on a specific scene in the play. On these occasions it is particularly useful not to prompt a player who dries, but instead to ask a few pertinent questions relating to the 'gone before' or the purpose of the character in that scene. Invariably the question is sufficient to remind the players of their lines, and they are less likely to forget in future.

Discipline at rehearsals is very important, but you need to impose this in a manner which will bring you respect. If you tackle your work in an efficient way, and you are prepared to give praise as well as adverse criticism, this respect will follow. People talk about the theatrical temperament, but I always remember one wise old Director on explaining that when tantrums were in evidence, it was usually 50% bad temper and 50% weakness of mentality.

Prompt and regular attendance at rehearsals and dedication to the production are the basics of a good company spirit. Respect should be there for other members and for their contribution to the production. This is shown by not allowing or creating distractions when they are rehearsing, by not making rude comments on their performances, by understanding the problems stage staff are facing in their efforts to supply the most suitable properties, costumes, etc.

In an amateur company, it is a wise Director who ensures that all are encouraged to undertake one of the back stage tasks. This makes for wider understanding of the difficulties that are met, and the process of overcoming such problems.

I have previously stated that it is unwise to try to tackle too large a section of that theatrical jigsaw puzzle in which you are involved. It's far better to ensure that the detail is firmly established before attempting to complete the picture.

For example, imagine a scene which needs to build up to a climax. It will most probably start with conversation at a normal level of tempo, with a character then expressing an opinion or revealing a painful truth. This creates a spark to the atmosphere and remarks are made which lead to a quarrel. The tempo is building throughout and the timing is of paramount importance. Equally important will be the decision as to which are the pertinent lines, those which must be heard, and which are the unimportant lines that technically can be 'thrown away'. Remember that, in a really heated quarrel, much is lost, though the basics underlying the argument still remain. It is often the *fact* that a strong argument is taking place that is important, rather than the minor detail of the dialogue.

Another aspect of performance which may need special attention is where a character who is involved in dialogue also has to cope with stage 'business'. A simple example is the pouring and serving of tea. How often I have seen the entire production come to a full stop while this action occurs. Yet, when carrying out such tasks in our own homes we do not cease all conversation! Therefore, it should be made clear from the start of rehearsals at which point of the dialogue the separate processes of the pouring and the serving of tea occur. Thus it is essential that 'props' supply the necessary equipment, including the liquid contents, at each rehearsal. Only by precise timing can the simplest task appear natural, and by such discipline the player gains confidence.

Yet another example of a tricky problem is when a stage fight is involved. Sword fights apart, which really need the choreography of an expert, a general principle is that it is the *attacked* who is the main protagonist, although the opposite impression is given to the audience.

e.g. (a) A 'strangler' will clasp hands round his victim's throat, but the only pressure he exerts is of his two thumbs against each other. At the same time his fingers at the back of the victim's neck will appear to show the strain through the knuckles. In the meantime, however, the 'victim' will choke, writhe about as if trying to escape, and maybe will even claw his way to the ground clutching madly at his attacker's body.

(b) During an assault, the impression may be given of fists coming in contact with flesh and bone, but the attacked one 'rides' the punches and makes the appropriate vocal reaction. Once the victim is on the ground, the attacker may kick hard to the stomach, but the foot actually stops within an inch of contact while the victim doubles up and moans in supposed agony.

These are two simple examples, yet they must be rehearsed carefully, so that all involved are aware of each movement and how it is co-ordinated with the text.

As the latter stage of rehearsal time approaches, it is advisable that all the sound effects are introduced, for they need timing and checking for volume levels. The cast, too, need to be aware of the significance of the sound.

A Director needs also to look and listen carefully for any signs of 'pre-empting'. Let me explain:

If the freshness of the production is to be retained, it is essential that each line of dialogue should be heard by the cast as if for the first time, and given a spontaneous reaction. Yet, familiarity with the text obviously occurs, and this often leads to a look of anticipation from a player turning to the character who has the next line. Sometimes there is a turn of the head to the door a split second before someone enters, or just prior to a doorbell being rung.

The player is awaiting the call, the ring of the bell, or the next sentence, and thus spontaneity is lost.

If you are dealing with a farce, such as *Hotel Paradiso*, *Boeing, Boeing* or *Who Goes Bare?*, you will surely be faced with a scene which includes a chase in and out of doors, a scene where the entrances and exits of certain characters need to be so carefully timed that they always *just* miss one another. If this involves a large cast, it requires technical precision from all concerned. It is a situation which must be studied so that each individual move is numbered.

In rehearsal, every move is made *slowly* until all are sure of their progress across the stage, and, perhaps back again. Only when all the players are absolutely certain of this should attempts be made to accelerate the action. To attempt to do this earlier is foolish and will only waste time.

This method will also work well when a tricky section of stage business has to be accomplished.

Once the 'pieces' are slotted together to complete a scene or an act, it is unwise to stop the momentum; far better to keep an ever-watchful eye and ear on any errors or weaknesses. The production secretary should be beside you, with your Director's script to hand, and prepared to take note of your comments. Unhampered, you are able to concentrate entirely on the developments of presentation, production and performances.

I would suggest that in the notepad used for this purpose, a wide column on one side is reserved for comments about the technical presentation and staging, and the remainder used for notes about the performances. By this method there is clarity between the two aspects of rehearsal, and the notes for the technicians can be mulled over with them once you have dealt with the cast.

All notes should be clearly given at the end of the section being rehearsed, and time spent on correcting the weaknesses.

If the production involves many scene changes, costume changes, and a complexity of properties, these will need to be rehearsed carefully and checked to assess the time taken.

The process may need speeding in some manner, for there is nothing more irritating for an audience than to be kept waiting for the continuation of the performance.

One method of doing a simple check is to involve the cast and technicians in a performance of just the opening and closing of each scene, what is known in the theatre as 'topping and tailing'. This will enable the S.M. to gain rudimentary knowledge of the running process, and of where the difficulties are likely to occur. These problems should be overcome before the final rehearsals. So often such details are left too late, and the old adage 'it'll be all right on the night' is trotted out. I do not believe in that principle, and prefer to do all that is humanly possible before the dress rehearsals commence.

On those occasions and during technical rehearsals you should hand over completely to your S.M., if you haven't already done so, and have a good look at the results of your labours. To ensure that nothing is missed, I would suggest you adopt the principles of an adjudicator.

Before proceeding, however, it would be a wise move to ensure that the cast are aware of certain aspects of backstage behaviour. While this is not really within the province of the Director, but of the S.M., it will affect the whole atmosphere and can, therefore, influence the success or failure of your production. While having 'fun' a company can lose a sense of professionalism which you have been trying to impart throughout rehearsals. It is worth following these simple, but vital, rules:

(a) The cast should never be seen in public while wearing either make-up or costume.
(b) The cast should not go on stage, even in the wings, until they have been 'called' by the S.M., and while

they are awaiting their cue they should not talk or create any distraction to other players or technicians.

(c) The cast should be aware of the regulations regarding fire prevention, and know what to do in the event of an emergency.

(d) The cast should ensure that all properties used are returned to the props department.

(e) The cast should see that costumes are replaced on hangers and not left in disarray.

(f) The cast should respect the accepted principle of 'no visitors' in dressing-rooms, either prior to, during or after a performance. Friends should be entertained elsewhere, once make-up and costumes are removed.

(g) The cast should leave dressing-rooms in a tidy condition, ready for the next performance.

(h) The cast should respect the authority of the S.M. at all times.

The whole company should be responsible for their personal property, and valuables should not be left unattended, or even brought to the theatre.

No doubt each company will have their own regulations, and while they may appear to be unnecessary, respect for the rules will, in the long run, create a happier atmosphere both back stage and in performance.

Chapter Fourteen

QUESTIONS OF ADJUDICATION

As final rehearsals draw near, the Director becomes so involved with the complexities of the task that it is sometimes difficult to assess exactly what has been achieved. Certainly you will be aware of the tasks that remain to be completed, and if you seek a high standard from everyone, there is never sufficient time to satisfy your demands.

You will be able to recognise the fact that each member of the cast has become two separate individuals; the player, and the person he or she is portraying. In the first instance you will be familiar with each player's temperament, talent and ability to use it to advantage, and with the amount of co-operation you have been given. In the second, you should be able to assess if all the character performances are fulfilling your expectations. Such knowledge will be invaluable in the future if you are likely to be directing these players in another production.

The technical staff should be very much in evidence, finalising the tasks they were set at that earlier meeting: the presentation of the show, and how it will look to the audience. Although administration is not within your terms of reference, an encouraging interest on your part will no doubt be appreciated. There is always the danger that with so many pieces of that 'jigsaw' to contend with, you will not see 'the wood for the trees'.

For slickness of presentation it is essential to hold technical rehearsals, and the preparations for these should be under the control of the Stage Manager. They know your requirements, and the lights should be rigged and set, sound apparatus placed in position and scene changes rehearsed without your presence being required. Here again our Production Secretary will prove invaluable, and should liaise with you in the event of any query. This is an opportunity for you to check on the wardrobe provided, and to examine the make-up ability of the cast. I firmly believe that any player should be capable of applying basic stage make-up, though more expertise must be gained before tackling difficult 'character' make-up.

Some experienced directors try to check all these points during the technical rehearsals, but it is not a practice I would recommend since I do not believe that details of make-up and wardrobe can be thoroughly studied in such circumstances.

Once the S.M. is confident that all is set according to the prepared plans, then you should give the technical team your undivided attention as they gradually work their way through the run of the cues. Stand-ins can be moved about the stage to check lighting areas, angles, and to ensure that there are no shadowy areas where they are not required. Levels of light and the effect of colour filters also need confirming.

You will also need to check the volume of sound effects and the music used to introduce or accompany the show, see how quickly and quietly the scenery is changed, and confirm the timing of the opening and closing of the tabs.

Once the technical rehearsal is over, it is advisable to sit down and discuss the weaknesses and strengths of the 'trial run' with all concerned, and do try to remember to thank everyone for their efforts. If there are any problems, a short re-run of 'topping and tailing' will often help to solve them.

This attitude of preparation may seem pedantic, but it is definitely preferable to that last minute rush, although I do appreciate that snags often occur which can create havoc. Everyone at this stage feels rather tense as they prepare to present the result of their labours to the general public, and there is less emotional upheaval if you can at least *appear* to be relatively calm and controlled.

Everyone looks to you for guidance, and in this final assessment and the giving of notes of appraisal and constructive criticism, it is better to try to achieve a workmanlike approach. It is unlikely that you are going to attain all your hopes and desires for this production, but much has been learnt by the way and will prove useful in the future.

Once the dress and final rehearsals are on stage, it is a supreme rule that *the stage is one area where you are not required*. You have done more or less all that it is possible for you to do, and the Stage Manager should be in firm control; any interference on your part is an affront to his or her authority.

You need to stay out of sight, give notes to your production secretary and let the show roll. Any final note-giving should be kept as short as possible, for everyone will be tired, and if you prolong the issue you defeat the object.

Don't forget to give the bouquets for good work, and if brickbats are necessary in some isolated instances try at least to be tactful and do it privately. A quiet word may work wonders, whereas a public slamming will only cause resentment.

As you sit and watch the show unfold, try to be your own judge, your own adjudicator. Be honest. Certain questions arise and notes should be made accordingly. What you are seeing is the result of your labours over the past weeks, your study, your planning, the manner in which you have handled the company, and whether or not you have been able to stretch their talents. At this late stage you will be bound to see certain things that you regret instigating, but rarely, and particularly with an amateur company, is it wise to try to change things. It all depends on the company and the change involved, but you can make sure that you don't repeat that mistake in future.

To begin with, take an honest look at the Presentation – and I make no apology for reiterating many factors which we have already discussed in previous chapters, or for including a few more examples for consideration.

Your review should commence with the dimming of the House Lights, the introductory music and the opening of the tabs. Is the introduction slick – the music, the sounds, the timing of the tabs, the first speech?

Is the set well-constructed, suitable in style, period and décor? Have you made intelligent use of the stage and its facilities? Has the convention of the play been reflected in the set design?

For instance, I recall that on one occasion I was adjudicating a play set in a small, dirty inn at the time of the Napoleonic Wars. The tabs opened to reveal not a small room, but the whole stage area of 40' x 30'. This was set with highly polished, obviously much-loved family antiques loaned by the cast. And therefore unsuitable. It would have been preferable to have used only the centre area of the stage. This could have been achieved by the partial closing of main tabs and traverse, and the lighting controlled to the centre area only. Dirty, plain wooden benches and barrels would have been more suitable for furniture, with the floor surface scattered with straw.

Another check on PROPERTIES will do no harm.

Are they correct in quantity, style and condition? Are they being handled with alacrity? Are there any anachronisms of period?

Again, I have seen a brown paper parcel, tied with nylon string, being discovered in a dungeon which had not been opened for over 200 years! I have seen modern matches being used to light a fire in a play set in 1600! I have seen a modern electric fire being used to warm a room in the Palace during the reign of Victoria!

And SOUND – Those opening effects . . . were they carefully faded out, or cut short with the loud click of the tape recorder? Were later effects timed with precision, sited to give authenticity to the sound? Was the scream credible, the slamming of the door consistent? Did that effect really sound like a car being driven away and then crashing? Some effects are better made manually, but there are excellent records made by the B.B.C., which can be a real asset.

LIGHTING – Was there careful co-ordination of lighting changes throughout the show? In general principle, the lighting should illuminate the play and not the scenery. Has this been achieved? There are, of course, variations of the principle when required by a theatrical situation. For example, in a play of tension, the silhouette of a character against an illuminated backcloth is often more effective than a face.

Has the source of light been considered? – the moonlight shining through a window, a standard lamp creating a pool of light, a fire creating lively shadows, and so on.

Do the colours used in the lamps, and the wattage of the bulbs, give the effect you seek? Are lighting changes precisely timed? for instance, the co-ordination of a lamp switched on by a member of the cast with the covering lamp control of the board operator; or the cross-fading of one area of light to another.

WARDROBE – When the cast entered, did they look like the reflections of the characters?

In a naturalistic production the *costumes* should be correct in style, period, condition, colour, quality and quantity, from what is worn on the head to the feet: that includes undergarments and the accessories carried. I recall that in the same production I discussed earlier, the one set in that small, dirty inn, the ladies of the cast arrived on stage looking beautiful, clean, well made-up, dresses well pressed but light and flimsy, a pretty sight indeed, very flattering. Yet, they had all 'travelled' overnight in a stage coach, suffering crowded conditions, and it was supposed to be the depths of winter.

Attention should be paid to the manner in which the garments are worn, for, with few exceptions, the cast should appear to be as familiar with their stage apparel as with their own everyday wear.

In a theatrical production, the players should be as comfortable as possible, but able to move about with the panache and style that the text requires.

Obviously, the more bizarre the design of the garments, the greater the effort required to be natural. Certainly familiarity is essential, though no director should expect miracles. Recently I read of an abortive London production where some of the dancers were expected to wear costumes created from small sections of glass. The blood ran freely and the cast rebelled!

MAKE-UP – The amount of make-up used depends on the type of play, the characters, and the strength of stage lighting. What you have to look for is an appearance which tells you that make-up has been used with discretion, to replace the natural colour that strong lighting has bleached out of the skin: an application which has created a character that the majority of the audience finds believable. It may appear to be more clearly defined to the front rows, but should not be obtrusive – though still sufficient to suggest line and shape to the people in the back rows of the theatre.

Again the questions. 'John Brown' has aged his face well to suggest the character, but what about his hands? Are they still youthful? Does that character make-up suggest years spent out in a hot climate? That one an alcoholic? That wig-join: does it show, or has it been carefully masked with make-up?

THE PERFORMANCES – Although you have been working with the cast from the onset, you must be prepared for the fact that once on that stage in view of the public they are really out of your hands, and there is often a tendency amongst players to 'embroider a canvas' which has already been accepted as complete. In most instances this is natural and desirable, for no performance is complete without the presence and reaction of the audience. They add a necessary dimension which brings the text to life and it is that dimension which makes the adrenalin flow and brings that vital spark so necessary to theatrical magic. What is to be deplored is an excess, a self-indulgent embroidery which can mar all that has been conceived through the long struggle or rehearsal. You will be blamed. So be prepared, and keep an ever watchful eye. Take this example:

An actor had been involved in constant discussion with me over the interpretation of a character in John Mortimer's play, *I Spy*. The actor was sure that the man was a homosexual. I was equally adamant that he was not. Eventually, the actor concurred and throughout rehearsals reacted accordingly. On the first performance, he 'camped up' the character mercilessly, and the critics slammed his performance!

So, to your general assessment of the cast. Are they audible, and are their speech patterns true to the characters they are portraying? Do they, by movement, stance and gesture, prove their understanding of the physical attributes of that character? Do the performances show a depth of feeling or are they mere façades of emotion? Do they, by their phrasing of the text, reveal the truth of purpose?

Are they facile in stage 'business'? Have they a natural stage presence and a confidence of movement around the locale with familiarity when required? Will they be able to add that necessary dimension to their performance, and yet be sensible enough not to fall into overplay? Are they in control of the text, and, if they 'dry', able to take a prompt with confidence? Have they truly created the developments within the situation, and demonstrated a wise sense of timing? Have they fulfilled the expectations you set them at that earlier stage of rehearsal?

You must accept that perfection in performance is rarely achieved, but if all the cast have used their talents to the best of their ability, and have shown that they have understood what you have been trying to do, then the result should not be scorned. Everyone will have learnt something about the art form during the course of the rehearsal period. You, perhaps, most of all. In the final summing up you must judge your own work, and in honesty accept the weaknesses as well as the strengths.

PRODUCTION – Have you managed to interpret the text according to your growing understanding of its purpose? If you have changed your opinion about some aspect of the play, have you managed to effect that change without distracting from the 'shape' of the play?

For instance, consider a play like *Once a Catholic* by Mary O'Malley. It is a play which tells of a simple Irish schoolgirl who, while she strives to be true to her faith, is bedevilled by distortions of the creed by her companions, is seduced in innocence and rejected by those from whom she seeks compassion and understanding. There is a great deal of bawdy and profane humour in the text. If the production leans too heavily on the humour, the satire and tragedy is lost. If the opposite interpretation is taken, then the humour is false. It is essential to retain the simplicity of the piece for the other elements to be retained in proportion.

Have you managed to define the Conflicts and Contrasts and to build the Climax unfalteringly? If the production falls into the genre of theatricality, have you created moments of magical fantasy, or is it rather prosaic without that special sparkle? If so, where do you think you may have erred in judgment?

Have you managed to obtain the maximum co-operation with your company? Has the production been a happy one, do they work as an ensemble? Do you think you will be asked to direct another show?

If so, what are the aspects of direction to which you need to give greater study? One can always learn, and should always be aware of the opportunities. In the following chapter, I give general information which should be useful to all who are interested in improving their knowledge of theatre.

When adjudicating, I say very frequently from the stage . . .

'YOUR FRIENDS WILL TELL YOU HOW GOOD YOU ARE . . . I HOPE THAT I CAN SHOW YOU HOW TO BE EVEN BETTER.'

I hope I have succeeded.

Chapter Fifteen

GENERAL INFORMATION

There is no reason why anyone interested in amateur theatre should complain about the scarcity of useful information. From magazines which have been specially published for enthusiasts of the art, to organisations both national and local, there is a multitude of advice about all aspects of theatre both amateur and professional.

The monthly magazine *Amateur Stage* covers a wide spectrum of amateur theatre both in Britain and abroad. Articles include reviews of the current professional scene, reviews of new books and plays, a theatre diary, and advice on various topics of practical interest. There is always the 'A Play Produced' section which deals with the approach of a director to a particular play, and would be of interest to anyone contemplating a similar production. This magazine can be obtained by subscription from:

Platform Publications Ltd
P.O. Box 1
St Albans, Herts. AL1 4ED

The magazine is very popular with theatre enthusiasts everywhere, and deservedly so. Charles Vance, the editor, has been a strong supporter of the amateur theatre for many years. For anyone seeking suitable material for productions there is a variety of sources apart from the professional publishers, the names of which are obtainable from the same publisher.

County libraries often have a Drama section with sets available for reading purposes on a fairly short loan. These sets should not be used for rehearsal and production since it is not possible to mark them with stage directions without diminishing their value: this is a practice which would be frowned upon by the librarian.

Some drama associations have stocks of plays, and these are also available to members on payment of a small charge. These organisations also contribute more than a library service to the amateur theatre.

Drama courses are invariably organised, some over a single weekend, others for longer periods, and nearly all of them run Summer Schools where, for an inclusive fee, players and technicians can join with others in a week-long session of tuition and production. These courses are usually held at a college or similar establishment, and often the opportunity is taken to visit the local professional theatre and to partake in activity which will stretch the student's knowledge of the art form.

THE THEATRE ASSOCIATION OF WALES offers similar services to members. They have an extensive library of plays and also have a hire service for lighting equipment, sound effect records and stage curtains and drapes. They run numerous courses in various locales, and their Newsletter gives notification of forthcoming productions by member groups. In addition to their Summer School, they are involved with a play-writing competition each year in an effort to encourage the work of new writers. Their address is:

1st Floor, Chapter Arts Centre, Market Rd., Canton, Cardiff.

Telephone: Cardiff (0222) 43794.

DRAMA ASSOCIATIONS IN IRELAND – Because of the complexities of the situation in Ireland, it is difficult to establish precisely the work of the many organisations that exist to support and aid the amateur theatre movement. There is no doubt that there is great enthusiasm for the art and generally a high standard is attained. The Drama Festivals that abound do much to bring theatre to a widespread audience. The following addresses are useful contacts:

ASSOCIATION OF ULSTER DRAMA FESTIVALS Co-ordinators of winners from Full-length Festivals in Ulster and organisers for the Finals of the 3 Act Festivals.

Secretary . . . Beth Duffin, 63 Seacourt Rd, Larne BT40 1TE

ULSTER ASSOCIATION OF AMATEUR DRAMA
General Manager, Group Theatre, Bedford Street, Belfast 1.

AMATEUR DRAMA COUNCIL OF IRELAND
Officer . . . Brendan O'Brien, 34, Beech Road, Athlone, Republic of Ireland.

This gentleman is also the Director of the All Ireland Festival held in Athlone.

AMATEUR DRAMA LEAGUE
Secretary . . . Catherine Leahy, 27, Victoria Road, Clontarf, Dublin 3, Ireland.

SCOTTISH COMMUNITY DRAMA ASSOCIATION (S.C.D.A.) Formed 1926.

Headquarters: Saltire House, 13, Atholl Crescent, Edinburgh, EH3 8HA.

Telephone (24 hour): 031 229 7838.

Aims: The development of amateur drama in Scotland, particularly on a community basis. The Association binds together amateur dramatic

144

societies throughout the country, and offers them advice, encouragement and practical help in the furtherance of their aims.

Director: Pru Kitching.

Membership: Open to any dramatic society in Scotland, and to any individual anywhere who sympathises with the aims of the Association.

Facilities/services provided for members:

1. Staff of professional drama tutors and professional producers available anywhere in Scotland.
2. Competitive Festivals for one-act and full-length plays in performance, professionally adjudicated, to encourage higher standards.
3. Five libraries of playscripts, technical books, etc.
4. Training courses and summer schools.
5. Youth theatre work.
6. International exchange between clubs.
7. Playwriting competitions, linked to public performances.
8. Annual conference.

This Association is a member of the International Amateur Theatre Association and the Central Council for Amateur Theatre.

Groups who may be interested in giving new writers an opportunity should certainly be aware of the work of an organisation known as NEW PLAYWRIGHTS' NETWORK.

This exciting project was launched in 1972 to publicise the works of new and highly talented writers awaiting recognition. Manuscripts of new plays, full-length and one-act, are appraised by an independent panel of enthusiastic readers who have specialised knowledge and who are keenly aware of the needs of the amateur theatre movement. The best scripts are then chosen for publication and are often available for reading from the major libraries throughout the United Kingdom. Copies are also available from the publishers and catalogues will be sent on request upon receipt of a s.a.e. Any writers who would be interested in submitting their manuscripts for consideration are asked to send a stamped addressed envelope for further details.

Concessions are allowed to members purchasing scripts from the leading publishers, and material and equipment from general theatre suppliers.

Membership of NEW PLAYWRIGHTS' NETWORK is currently £1 only.

Address: 35, Sandringham Road, Macclesfield, Cheshire, SK10 1QB.

Telephone: 0625 25312.

In Chapter 3 I mentioned a publisher who deals in second-hand play scripts. I should make it quite clear that Peter Wood also deals in new publications and has a comprehensive list of all theatre books: this is available on request.

Address: 20, Stonehill Road, Great Shelford, Cambridge, CB2 5JL.

Publishers can supply catalogues of play scripts, and these are usually dealt with in specialised sections such as the following:

One-Act Plays: for Mixed Casts
for Youth Groups
for All Women
for All Men

HOW TO PRODUCE A PLAY

Full-Length Plays: for Mixed Casts
                             for Youth Groups
                             for All Women
                             for All Men

Revue Material.
Pantomimes.
Plays with a Religious Theme.

If your theatre group would like to arrange a drama course on their own premises, but are not sure how to contact a tutor who is well versed in the theatre, I cannot do better than to suggest that you write to the GUILD OF DRAMA ADJUDICATORS. Each adjudicator *who is a member of that organisation* has had to face a stringent test of their knowledge and ability in theatre art, and many are willing to tutor such a course on a chosen subject. They are all very experienced and aware of the problems facing the amateur theatre, though many of them have had training in the professional theatre.

The specified objects of the Guild are:

To supply qualified adjudicators to all organisations promoting amateur drama.

To foster and protect the interests of its members.

To provide opportunities for discussions and tuition either by schools, conferences or by other means.

The Secretary of the Guild will forward, upon enquiry, a Directory of the membership which includes details of their particular interests and the extent of their experience. This Directory is issued yearly.

Secretary: Mrs Jessica Eyre, 34 Harwood Road, Marlow, Bucks. SL7 2AS (06284 74718)

The ability to assess your own production would be considerably increased by regular attendance at Drama Festivals, and by entering them when at all possible.

At such Festivals an experienced adjudicator will, after having studied the play in depth, and after taking stock of the resources available to the teams, sit in constructive judgement on the performance and production. A public review is then given, with suggestions made as to how the weaker aspects could be improved, and praise given for the achievements that have been made.

Most areas have Drama Festivals at some time during the year, and I know that much can be learnt by watching and listening to this qualified assessment.

THE NATIONAL DRAMA FESTIVALS ASSOCIATION was formed in May, 1964. Its objects . . .

1. To encourage and support the amateur theatre in all its forms and in particular, the Drama Festival.
2. To bring together at conferences these organisations and individuals to discuss matters of common interest.
3. To encourage the playwright in the writing of plays by sponsoring playwriting competitions, and to organise the production and publication of works of entertainment.
4. To feed member Festivals with information by means of a Festival Newsletter at regular intervals.
5. To raise the standard of Drama Festivals by organising an ALL WINNERS Festival.
6. To negotiate with other bodies as a collective force on behalf of member Festivals.
7. To act as a liaison between Festivals requiring emergency help.
8. To issue a Year Book in January of each year.

Chairman: Brenda Nicholl, 24, Jubilee Road, Formby, Liverpool, L37 2HT.

Groups whose main interest lies in the field of Musical Drama would be advised to seek membership of the following society, whose knowledge and experience of Stage musicals give so much support to this activity.

NATIONAL OPERATIC AND DRAMATIC
ASSOCIATION
1, Crestfield Street, London, WC1 8AU.
Telephone: 01 837 5655.

Its services include an extensive library of musical scores, libretti and plays, the organisation of Summer Schools for Operatic and Dramatic Training, and the publication of a Bulletin for up-to-date news of events.

Those seeking specialised information about performance in Church, or wishing to obtain scripts with a religious theme can find useful information from:

RADIUS: RELIGIOUS DRAMA SOCIETY OF
GREAT BRITAIN
George Bell House, Bishop's Hall, Ayre Street, London, S.E.1.